£10.00

What's

in Shakespeare's

Names

"Shakspeare [*sic*] and His Friends," engraving by James Faed after painting by John Faed in the Corcoran Gallery of Art, Washington, D.C.

What's
in Shakespeare's
Names

by

Murray J. Levith

London

G E O R G E   A L L E N   &   U N W I N

Sydney

First published in 1978
in the United States of America
as an Archon Book, an imprint of The Shoe String Press, Inc.
Hamden, Connecticut 06514,
and in Great Britain by
George Allen & Unwin (Publishers) Ltd.

British Library Cataloguing in Publication Data

Levith, Murray J.
    What's in Shakespeare's names.
    1.   Shakespeare, William - Characters
    I.   Title
    822.3'3   PR2989
ISBN 0-04-822039-6

Printed in the United States of America

for Tina

CONTENTS

PREFACE

A careful reader is always on the alert for directions—"clues" the author gives to intention and meaning. One such clue is to be found in deliberately named characters, a common practice of writers throughout literary history. Although some of Shakespeare's characters have obviously significant names, it is relatively recent that any attempt has been made to study this aspect of the playwright's craft.

The aim of my book is to provide a helpful handle to Shakespeare, perhaps even refine our understanding of authorial tone in the plays. I begin with a chapter of introduction, noting what has been said in the past about names in Shakespeare, and forwarding some generalizations about the playwright's naming practices. The next three chapters detail character names in each of the thirty-seven plays: Histories, Tragedies, and Comedies and Romances. The order of the chapters is dictated by Shakespeare's increasing inventiveness as he becomes less bound to source materials. Not every name in a given play is significant, and so I have commented selectively. The reader will find, however, that most, and sometimes all, names in a play are addressed. My last chapter is about Shakespeare's own name.

There is redundancy resulting from explaining examples in the introductory chapter, and then dealing with these names again as they come up in the individual plays. Since some readers may wish to use the middle chapters as a sort of glossary, seeking information on one particular play, it seemed wiser to repeat rather than redirect.

G. Blakemore Evans has edited the most up-to-date (and easy to obtain) one-volume text with standard line numberings; hence, *The Riverside Shakespeare* is used for quotations and spellings. This edition also serves as the basis for Marvin Spevack's *Complete and Systematic Concordance to the Works of Shakespeare.* There is, however, a drawback to *The Riverside Shakespeare:* the departure from some of the traditional spellings of character names without, it seems to me, sufficient reason in every case. I have overlooked this deficiency.

A study of this kind inevitably evolves. Obviously I have tried to be as careful and complete as possible, but readers with, say, more linguistic, historical, or Shakespearean expertise will come along to clarify, expand, or perhaps even confute my specific observations. Indeed, I am certain that my own views on some of Shakespeare's names will modify or change. I welcome all refinements warmly.

ACKNOWLEDGMENTS

My first debt of gratitude for the realization of this book is to the people of Grossweil, Bavaria, West Germany. Without the warmth and friendliness of butcher Frau Schmid, baker Frau Luidl, garage mechanic Herr Fichtner, and Post lady Fräulein Leis, the initial draft would have taken considerably longer to write. Our next-door neighbors, the *Familie* Steingruber, mostly laughed but also cried with my wife and me for the good part of a year. *"Nun bin I a Bayer."*

Professor Dr. Wolfgang Clemen of the University of Munich permitted me to use the Shakespeare library of the *Englische Seminar,* and helped locate hard-to-find German materials relating to my study. My good friends at the Skidmore College Library were most efficient in tracking down articles and books not in our own library. Dr. O.B. Hardison, Jr., and the staff of the Folger Shakespeare Library, Washington, D.C., made doing research away from "home" a genuine pleasure.

Skidmore College granted me a sabbatical leave to work on this book, and the Skidmore College Faculty Research Grants

Committee was generous with a summer stipend as my writing neared completion. My colleague and friend Dr. Helga Doblin read the manuscript. Mary L. Willey and Pamela Nelson helped with proofreading.

The late Professor T.M. Raysor of the University of Nebraska would always read Falstaff's lines with a twinkle in his eye, and his inspired teaching ignited my own consuming interest in Shakespeare.

Most of all, Tina.

What's

in Shakespeare's

Names

The poet's eye, in a fine frenzy rolling,
Doth glance from heaven to earth, from earth to heaven;
And as imagination bodies forth
The forms of things unknown, the poet's pen
Turns them to shapes, and gives to aery nothing
A local habitation and a name.

A Midsummer Night's Dream (V,i,12-17)

O Romeo, Romeo, wherefore art thou Romeo?

Romeo and Juliet (II,ii,33)

1   JULIET'S QUESTION

Some of Shakespeare's most familiar lines occur during the balcony scene in *Romeo and Juliet* when Juliet asks a hidden Romeo to "refuse" his name. "'Tis but thy name that is my enemy," she reasons. "O, be some other name!"[1] There follows Juliet's famous question: "What's in a name?"

Her equally famous answer is nothing's in a name:

> That which we call a rose
> By any other word [Quarto 1 has "name"] would smell as
> sweet;
> So Romeo would, were he not Romeo call'd,
> Retain that dear perfection which he owes
> Without that title.   (II,ii,43-47)

Juliet to the contrary, however, names mean a lot—and certainly in Shakespeare.

Books explaining names in the Classics and the Bible began appearing in England toward the end of the fifteenth century. Late in the sixteenth, one William Patten published his exhaustively titled *The Calender of Scripture, Wherein the Hebru, Calldian, Arabian, Phenician, Syrian, Persian, Greek and Latin names, of*

This chapter appeared in somewhat different form in *Renaissance and Modern: Essays in Honor of Edwin M. Moseley,* edited by Murray J. Levith (Saratoga Springs, N.Y.: Skidmore College, 1976).

Nations, Cuntreys, Men, Weemen, Idols, Cities; Hils, Riuers, & of
oother places in the holly Byble mentioned, by order of letters ar set,
and turned into oour English Toong (STC 19476). In his "Praefatio"
to *De Sapientia Veterum,* Francis Bacon explains that the ancients
chose names for the characters of their fables most deliberately:
"cum Metis uxor Jovis plane consilium sonet; Typhon tumorem;
Pan universum; Nemesis vindictam: et similia."[2] Elizabethan and
Jacobean dramatists were often obvious with character names, as for
example Ben Jonson in *Volpone.* William Camden's 1605 edition of
Remaines of a Greater Worke, Concerning Britaine (STC 4521) and
the 1607 revision of *Britannia* (STC 4508) included glossaries to
explain both men's and women's names from Anglo-Saxon,
Hebrew, Greek, and Latin roots. Camden observes in *Remaines*
"that names among all nations and tongues . . . are significative, and
not vaine senselesse sounds." He cites examples even to "the
barbarous Turks, . . . the savages of *Hispaniola* and all *America,"* and
"they of *Congo."* Thus, he concludes, "it were grosse ignorance and
to no small reproach of our Progenitours, to thinke their names
onely nothing significative, because that in the daily alteration of our
tong, the signification of them is lost, or not commonly knowne" (p.
36).

   Not until the nineteenth century, however, does the deliberateness of Shakespeare's names begin to attract notice. Perhaps
this aspect of the playwright's art seemed too obvious to mention
earlier. In any event, in December of 1862 John Ruskin published
sections from his *Munera Pulveris,* a treatise on political economy,
which in asides and footnotes attempts to explain the significance of
some of Shakespeare's names. Ruskin notes that names in Shakespeare "are curiously—often barbarously—much by Providence,—
but assuredly not without Shakespeare's cunning purpose—mixed
out of the various traditions he confusedly adopted, and languages
which he imperfectly knew."[3] Focusing on etymology, Ruskin explains Desdemona as meaning "miserable fortune," Othello as "the
careful," Ophelia "serviceableness," Hamlet "homely," Hermione
"pillar-like," Titania "the queen," Benedick and Beatrice "blessed"
and "blessing," Valentine and Proteus "enduring" and "changeful,"
and Iago and Iachimo [Jachimo] both "the supplanter." In another
section, Ruskin relates Portia to "fortune's lady," Perdita to "lost

lady," and Cordelia to "heart-lady." Ruskin promised a full-length study of Shakespeare's names at some later date, but it never materialized. Perhaps the reason was Matthew Arnold's scathing criticism of his first efforts.

Arnold responded to Ruskin's excursions with feigned or real outrage. In *The Cornhill Magazine,* he summarizes Ruskin's observations on Shakespeare's names with a sentence of dismissal: "Now really, what a piece of extravagance all that is!"[4] Taking Ruskin to task for faulty etymologies and particularly for giving nomenclature undue prominence, Arnold accuses Ruskin of being unbalanced and, undoubtedly worst of all, provincial. Perhaps this severity of rebuke deterred all but the most passing critical interest in Shakespeare's names until quite recently.

Several prominent twentieth-century novelists, however, have evinced fascination with names in Shakespeare. James Joyce, for example, finds the biographical associations of several character names from the plays noteworthy. In *Ulysses,* Stephen Dedalus argues that Shakespeare's "mother's name lives in the forest of Arden." Further, says Stephen, "He had three brothers, Gilbert, Edmund, Richard. Gilbert . . . is nowhere: but an Edmund and a Richard are recorded in the works of sweet William. . . . In his trinity of black Wills, the villain shakebags, Iago, Richard Crookback Edmund in *King Lear,* two bear the wicked uncles' names. Nay, that last play was written or being written while his brother Edmund lay dying in Southwark." Stephen also plays memorably with the playwright's and his wife's own names: "If others have their will Ann hath a way."[5]

Vladimir Nabokov's *Bend Sinister* contains a scene with the characters Krug and Ember discussing the names in *Hamlet* with reference to themes. "Krug suggests tampering with Hamlet's name. . . . Take 'Telemachos,' he says, which means 'fighting from afar'—which again was Hamlet's idea of warfare. Prune it, remove the unnecessary letters, all of them secondary additions, and you get the ancient 'Telmah.' Now read it backwards. Thus does a fanciful pen elope with a lewd idea and Hamlet in reverse gear becomes the son of Ulysses slaying his mother's lovers." Ember contends that the name Ophelia "can be derived from that of an amorous shepherd in Arcadia. Or quite possibly it is an anagram of Alpheios, with the 'S' lost in the damp grass—Alpheus the rivergod, who pursued a long-legged nymph until Artemis changed her into a stream, which of course suited his liquidity to a tee. . . . Or again we can base it on the Greek rendering of an old Danske serpent name. . . . Ophelia, serviceableness. Died in passive service." In like manner, "Polonius-Pantolonius, a pottering dotard in a padded robe, shuffling about in carpet slippers and following the sagging spectacles at the end of his nose, as he waddles from room to room." Or, of Yorick and Osric: "Hamlet has just been speaking to the skull of a jester; now it is the skull of jesting death that speaks to Hamlet. Note the remarkable juxtaposition: the skull—the shell; 'Runs away with a shell on his head.' Osric and Yorick almost rhyme, except that the yolk of one has become the bone (os) of the other. Mixing as he does the language of the shop and the ship, this middleman, wearing the garb of a fantastic courtier, is in the act of selling death, the very death that Hamlet has just escaped at sea."[6]

G. Wilson Knight revives critical interest in Juliet's question with a chapter in *The Sovereign Flower,* and his study is provocative and often insightful.[7] He notices, for example, the power conveyed by the *o*'s in Oberon, Morocco, Othello, Orsino and, conversely, the "certain lightness" of "Ophelia's name, with its rising vowel-sounds from 'o' through 'e' to 'i'." Knight is always interesting even when he seems far afield, as with Yorick and Osric. He writes that contained in these names "may be an overtone of 'joke': one *made* jokes, the other *is* a joke."

Harry Levin has written another chapter on the subject.[8] In it he acknowledges the worth of Knight's study, though recognizing its limitations. Levin is a bit more careful than Knight, but in the end goes over much the same ground. Levin's essay does, however, offer an appealing invitation for further study of Juliet's question: "Except for one or two German dissertations [perhaps Ernst Erler, *Die Namengebung bei Shakespeare,* Heidelberg, 1913, and Wilhelm Oelrich, *Die Personennamen im Mittelalterlichen Drama Englands,* Kiel, 1911], which are hardly more than annotated listings, plus a few articles on specific lines of derivation, the field of Shakespearean nomenclature is wide open, and constitutes an inviting pasture to browse in."

Shakespeare himself is on record about the poetic process

18

in *A Midsummer Night's Dream:* the poet "gives to aery nothing/ A local habitation and a name" (V,i,16-17). The word "name" here is literal as well as general in meaning. A character's name can create an image both dramatic and poetic. This is not to say that every one of Shakespeare's names is meaningful or significative. It does little good to "find" meaning where none has been implied or intended. On the other hand, names are often tonal and can provide significant reading directions—clues to thematic meanings and characterizations. In some plays Shakespeare was limited by names inherited from source materials. Nevertheless, in such instances he might build characterization consistent with the suggestiveness of a received name. Hotspur comes first to mind in this regard. Presumably Shakespeare read the name in Holinshed's *Chronicles* and then created the volatile personality to go with it. The playwright's invented names, too, are often similarly linked to characterization. This is easiest to observe in his denotative or "tag" names.

For the most part dealing with minor and especially comic characters and secondary play actions, Shakespeare will single out a vivid attribute and so label a character, either by occupation, physical trait or feature, or some notable aspect of personality.

Sir Oliver *Martext* is a country priest, and the Mistresses Quickly, Overdone, and Doll Tearsheet are named with allusions to their bawdy business. Abhorson is a portmanteau of *abhor* and *whoreson,* apt for an executioner. Another executioner, Richard II's, is Sir Pierce (of Exton). Brakenbury (*break* and *bury*) is the Lieutenant of the Tower in *Richard III.*

Some of the thieving crew in the *Henry IV* plays also have occupational tag names. Gadshill is from the location of robbery, Gads Hill in Kent. Peto suggests *petard,* literally a 'small weapon,' like a Pistol, another character's name. Fang's name means 'capture,' and so he does Falstaff, aided by Snare.

As well as occupations, the "rude mechanicals" of *A Midsummer Night's Dream,* Snout, Starveling, Bottom, and Quince, are named for intended physical features. Snout is presumably long-nosed, Starveling has a thin physique, and Bottom a broad seat. Quince might be small and wizened like the fruit.

Other characters in Shakespeare are similarly designated. Dr. Pinch has a slight build, as do Sir Andrew Aguecheek and

Slender, who is thin of both girth and wit. Justice Shallow is named for his mental endowment, and so are Simple and Simpcox. Silence doesn't speak much. And, of course, Sir Toby.

Most of the tag names in the plays are English. But the setting of *All's Well That Ends Well* is at times French, and we find in this play a 'fiery' Lafew and 'wordy' Parolles. Even when a setting isn't French, one may have a "strong-armed" Fortinbras, or a French queen Cordelia with a noble 'heart of a lion.' When the setting is Italian, we encounter the 'blond' Biondello or the 'white' and 'pure' Bianca of *The Taming of the Shrew*. Malvolio is ill-willed and Benvolio is good-willed in keeping with their names.

Shakespeare creates a special group of tag names in the Romances, the meanings of which are explained in the plays themselves. Miranda denotes the 'one to be admired or wondered at,' so Ferdinand addresses his love at one point as "Admir'd Miranda" (III,i,37) and at another exclaims "O you wonder!" (I,ii,427). Marina, in *Pericles,* explains that she was "Call'd Marina/ For I was born at sea" (V,i,155-156). In *The Winter's Tale,* Hermione asks that her newly born be named Perdita, "for the babe/ Is counted lost for ever" (III,iii,32-33).

Tag names are used at times ironically in terms of character. The play *Othello* seems consciously structured with irony in mind—black is good, white is bad—and in it is a courtesan Bianca. Angelo of *Measure for Measure* is surely no angel, and neither is Juliet's garrulous nurse Angelica. We might expect a sharper Launce than we get in *The Two Gentlemen of Verona;* rather dull also is Launcelot Gobbo.

One other sort of denotative name occurs in Shakespeare. While Seyton is a legitimate Scottish clan name, it is homonymous with the devil's designation. As the central character in a psycho-machian allegory, Macbeth has lost his soul to the forces of Evil, and it is most appropriate for him to have Seyton (Satan) as his attendant. Another character named in the manner of the old allegories and moralities is Patience, "woman" to noble Queen Katherine in *Henry VIII*.

Unfortunately not all of Shakespeare's tag names are obvious to the modern reader or playgoer. In some cases, significant denotation has become obscured owing to normal language change and can be recovered only with the help of historical dictionaries. Nym's name, for example, under *nim* in the *O.E.D.*, meant 'to steal' in colloquial jargon; in *Henry V* Nym is reported hanged for just this crime.

With foreign names the problem of tag meanings is compounded. John Florio's copious Italian/English dictionary *A Worlde of Wordes* (STC 11098) and its expanded editions are helpful for Italian names.[9] Florio was tutor to the Earl of Southampton, Shakespeare's patron, and perhaps best known for his translation of Montaigne's *Essays*.[10] He explains the word *stéfano* in part as follows: "hath bin used in jest for a mans bellie, panch, craver, mawe, or gut," and this definition helps to tag the character Stephano's physical appearance. A clue to how a character might be played in terms of his given name is also suggested by the dictionary. Thus we have *peto,* "one that doth lightly roule his eies with a grace from corner to corner, goat-eied, rouling-eied. Also he that looketh as his eies were halfe closed, or he that looketh asquint upward." The word *bardo* as "light, nimble, bould, saucie" similarly points to a possible personality for Shakespeare's thief.

William Camden's glossaries, too, are contemporary aids for establishing what a name might have suggested to the playwright or his audience. Camden defines Edgar as "*Happy,* or *blessed honor,* or *power,*" and Oswald as "House-ruler or Steward" (*Remaines,* pp. 50, 65). Postdating Shakespeare, but at times useful as well, is Edward Lyford's 1655 edition of *The true Interpretation and Etymologie of Christian Names* (Wing L3543). E. G. Withycombe's *The Oxford Dictionary of English Christian Names*[11] is an enormous help, as are standard Greek and Latin dictionaries.

Some of Shakespeare's character names allude to similarly named figures in mythology, literature, the Bible, history, or some other familiar source. Such allusion serves oftentimes to delineate character rapidly or may have a comic function. Autolycus, Mercury's thieving son in Ovid, explains himself as such in *The Winter's Tale:* "My father nam'd me Autolycus, who being, as I am, litter'd under Mercury, was likewise a snapper-up of unconsider'd trifles" (IV,iii,24-26). The juxtaposition of Rowland, Orlando, and Oliver in *As You Like It* recalls the famous *Chanson de Roland.* Aaron and Jessica are Old Testament names, and both characters are aliens in their plays. Shakespeare was especially fond of giving his servants out-sized allusive names. Thus we find Sampson in *Romeo and Juliet,* and Alexander in *Troilus and Cressida.* Another comic device was to afford characters oxymoronic names—fine ones contradicted by mean ones. Here we might list Christopher Sly, Anthony Dull, and Pompey Bum, among others. For these names, Shakespeare's typical pattern is to couple an allusion in the Christian name with a denotative tag in the family name.

The playwright gives animal names to some of his characters, and these can be denotative, allusive, or both. Lavatch corresponds to the French words for 'the cow,' and Dogberry, while literally referring to the fruit of the dogwood tree, also recalls the animal. Talbot suggests the hunting hound, ancestor of the bloodhound. The names Tybalt and Reynaldo are both to be found in the medieval story of *Reynard the Fox:* Tybalt is the cat, and Reynaldo is the sly fox himself. Petruchio's successful wooing changes Kate from a "wildcat" to a delicate "cate."

In 1596 Sir John Harington published a widely circulated Rabelaisian book with the innocent title *The Metamorphosis of Ajax* (STC 12779).[12] Among other things, the book is an announcement of the flush toilet, which Harington refers to as "a jax." The name Ajax soon became synonymous with privy in the contemporary idiom. Foul smells associated with privies were thought to induce melancholy, and Shakespeare's Ajax in *Troilus and Cressida* is described as "melancholy without cause" (I,ii,26). The same name association obtains for Jaques in *As You Like It* and Jaquenetta, a feminine diminutive of *Jaques,* in *Love's Labor's Lost.* The English Jack is the popular nickname for John, still slang for toilet. Thus Don John in *Much Ado About Nothing* may be deliberately named with a glance at his temperament. Iago, Spanish for James, is another variant (see Camden's *Remaines,* p. 59), and this name might be thought to link the character's disposition for evil with melancholy. Jachimo, a diminutive of Iago, is similar, containing a clue to the character's temperament.

With recent history, allusion was not always without hazards: Oldcastle's descendants were alive to complain and necessitate a name change. In *The Merry Wives of Windsor,* Brook is an appropriate wet alias for Ford, but the name had to be watered down to a dry Broome for the Folio to avoid offending the Seventh Lord Cobham, William *Brooke*. Ancient history, too, could inhibit creativity if classical tradition dictated that Cressida might only be Cressida.

On the other hand, there was room for great allusive subtlety. The name Theseus in *A Midsummer Night's Dream* triggers recollection of the Minotaur myth. In Shakespeare's play, Bottom, the fabulous ass-man, is found at the center of a forest-labyrinth containing some "lost" young people. Invited to get to the "bottom" of "this most rare vision" of plays within plays and dreams within dreams, Shakespeare's audience need clutch only at the thread of the meaning of Bottom's name—a weaver's spool, which Theseus used to defeat the Minotaur.

Similarly, a saint's legend might be invoked with a given name and have interpretive value for a play. In *The Merchant of Venice,* for example, the title character's name recalls two well-known saints, Saint Anthony the Great and Saint Anthony of Padua. According to legend, Saint Anthony the Great, like Antonio the merchant, had remarkable patience when confronting various trials, and he led an ascetic life. Even closer to Shakespeare's play perhaps is the other Saint Anthony's story. In addition to his fame as patron of the poor (as the generous merchant is for Bassanio), his life contains a central episode concerning the conversion of a heretic.

Henry VIII affords another example of allusive subtlety. Here Shakespeare uses source names from history, but exploits them in a manner which enriches the thematic material of his play. Anne Bullen's Christian name is the same as Saint Ann, mother of the Virgin Mary. Anne's child Elizabeth, then, is associated through allusion with the Virgin Queen of Heaven. Elizabeth, of course, was remembered by the audience for *Henry VIII* as the Virgin Queen of Earth.

Finally, *King John* provides one further illustration of name allusion in Shakespeare's plays. John has not been especially favored among English kings. Richard and Henry seem the most popular royal names, especially for the periods of history Shakespeare treats in his plays. Arthur has particularly potent mythic associations. These four names are all to be found in *King John*. The reason is that one of Shakespeare's themes in the play is kingship in its various aspects. John is the designation for a bad king, Richard (recalling the Lionhearted) for a brave one, Arthur for the legendary, and Henry for the good governor of a great empire. The Bastard changes his given name Philip, associated more with French than English kings, to Richard after his supposed father Richard the Lionhearted.

Shakespeare's own name is composed of double English syllables, *shake* and *spear,* and a number of the playwright's characters have similarly formulated names: Falstaff, Hotspur, Shylock, Touchstone. What is remarkable here is the importance to their plays of the characters so named. None is a protagonist, but all are central figures.

What about some of the more poetic aspects of Shakespearean nomenclature? A reader merely rehearsing the *Dramatis Personae* of *Othello*—Othello, Desdemona, Iago, Cassio—knows from the sounds of the names that this will not be a comedy. A chorus of women is suggested by the alliterated names in *Coriolanus:* Valeria, Virgilia, Volumnia. Another is to be found in *A Midsummer Night's Dream:* Hippolyta, Hermia, and Helena. Shakespeare also exploits alliteration in order to juxtapose characters for comparison or contrast: Hotspur and Hal, Edgar and Edmund, Richard and Richmond, Macbeth and Macduff, Benedick and Beatrice. The indistinguishable false friends of Hamlet are Rosencrantz and Guildenstern whose names jingle together. Richard II's favorites, Bushy, Bagot, and Green, have names which, taken together with the mentioned but not seen Wiltshire, suggest an uncared for garden. In *Henry V,* the Welsh Fluellen, the Irish MacMorris, and the Scottish Jamy are meant to reflect the diversity of King Henry's subjects and suggest a British microcosm.

While patterns in Shakespeare's naming of characters can be observed and analyzed, there also arise some baffling questions to which satisfactory answers may never be forthcoming. Why, for example, are there two Jaques and two Olivers in *As You Like It?* Why two dissimilar characters in a play both with the name Bardolph? Why a conjuror with Henry IV's family name? Why two Eglamours? Why a minor middle man Claudio when Claudius is such an important character in *Hamlet?* Why so many Antonios in the plays? Why so many names beginning with the syllable *Luc-?*

24

As the nurse tells us, Juliet is named for her birth month (see I,iii,21), and we have left her poised on the balcony with her question. We recall she has asked the still hidden Romeo to "doff" his offendingly meaningful name. "Who's there," Juliet wants to know when she hears something below. The perplexed Romeo can only respond amusingly: "By a name,/ I know not how to tell thee who I am" (II, ii, 53-54).

2   HISTORIES

Although the King is always the titular character, he is not always the central actor in Shakespeare's History Plays. The King is usually surrounded by a goodly number of named and titled nobles: there are never fewer than fifteen characters and as many as fifty speaking parts. In the History Plays, Shakespeare is most bound by his chronicle sources, but this does not prevent him from playing with inherited names. The underplots, however, allow him the most room to create characters and names for them. It is in these secondary and often comic actions where the most significant name play occurs.

Henry VI, Part 1

JOAN DE PUCELLE

Joan of Arc is Joan de Pucelle in the first part of *Henry VI*. With this designation, Shakespeare means to debunk the French saint and tag the morally loose character he has drawn for her. The word *pucelle,* 'maid or virgin,' from Medieval French, is a pun on *puzzel,* 'whore.'[1] The English hero Talbot makes the association explicit in the play: "Pucelle or puzzel, Dolphin or dogfish,/ Your [French] hearts I'll stamp out with my horse's heels" (I, iv, 107-108). The supposed maiden Joan pleads pregnancy when faced with execution (see V, iv, 59-64), and even her own father labels her "drab" (V, iv, 32).

Although Shakespeare's sister was a Joan, he clearly viewed the name as rustic and vulgar. In *King John,* for example, the bastard Faulconbridge boasts after his being dubbed as a knight: "Well, now can I make any Joan a lady" (I, i, 184). Berowne, too, contrasts the high-born with the lowly Joan in *Love's Labor's Lost:* "Some men must love my lady, and some Joan" (III, i, 205). And, at the end of the same play, it is "greasy Joan [who] doth keel the pot" in the song. The second part of *Henry VI* has "old Joan" as the name of a hawk (II, i, 4).

By way of contrast, the English Talbot's name has positive connotations. In *Henry V,* it is invoked by the King in his Saint Crispin's speech (IV, iii, 54). The name recalls the fierce hunting hound, ancestor of the present-day bloodhound. The character Talbot observes proudly that the French "call'd us for our fierceness English dogs" (I, v, 25). Indeed, the Bastard of Orleance views the fiery soldier as a hellhound: "I think this Talbot be a fiend of hell" (II, i, 46). Geoffrey Chaucer names a dog Talbot in "The Nun's Priest's Tale" (l. 563). Basset is another English dog in the play, but Shakespeare takes no special notice of his name.

A whelp who is ever running away (see I, v, 26) is Sir John Falstaff (traditionally spelled *Fastolfe* in this play from Theobald's edition onward). He is reported as cowardly and "fast off" from battle:

> Here had the conquest fully been seal'd up,
> If Sir John Falstaff had not play'd the coward.
> He, being in the vaward, plac'd behind
> With purpose to relieve and follow them [Talbot's forces],
> Cowardly fled, not having struck one stroke.   (I,i,130-134)

Talbot strips Falstaff of his Order of the Garter with these words:

> This dastard, at the battle of Poictiers,
> When, but in all, I was six thousand strong

TALBOT

BASSET

FALSTAFF

And that the French were almost ten to one,
Before we met, or that a stroke was given,
Like to a trusty squire did run away.   (IV, i, 19-23)

In response to a Captain's, "Whither away, Sir John Falstaff, in such
haste?", he replies incredulously and ignobly, "Whither away? to
save myself by flight" (III, ii, 104-105).

REIGNIER   The only other potentially significant name in the play is
the tag for the historical Duke of Anjou. Reignier is apt for the
titular King of Naples, but Shakespeare shows no concern with it.

Henry VI, Part 2

        Shakespeare creates an important low-life action in the
second part of *Henry VI,* and by doing so affords himself rich
CADE   opportunity for character invention and name play. Cade is an
historical personage, but his name is nonetheless significant. The
Latin *cade* means 'fall.' There are a number of quibbles on this
meaning in the play's dialogue. George Bevis and John Holland "fall
in" (IV, ii, 30) with a Cade who predicts that their common
"enemies shall [fall] before" them (IV,ii,35). Cade later confronts a
messenger of ill-tidings with: "Stand, villain, stand, or I'll fell thee
down" (IV, ii, 115). In this same scene, Cade's name provides the
occasion for several English puns by Dick the butcher. He plays on
the meaning of *cade* as 'herring barrel' (IV, ii, 33), and its sound
similarity with *cage* a few lines later (IV, ii, 52). Dick further
interprets Cade's claim to be a Mortimer with a knowing pun on this
name: "a good bricklayer" (IV, ii, 40-41).
        In fact, Cade is reported a "shearman" (IV, ii, 133) (cutter
of wool nap) and a "clothier" (IV, ii, 4). Thus he puns with some
SAY   authority on the title Lord Say, "say" being a kind of silk cloth: "Ah,
thou say, thou serge, nay, thou buckram lord!" (IV, vii, 25). The

progression is to cheaper material, as "serge" is wool and "buckram" a kind of linen. Cade's follower Holland may be similarly named for the linen fabric manufactured in the Netherlands and alluded to by the Hostess in *Henry IV, Part 1* (III, iii, 71).

HOLLAND

It has been noted, however, that the names John Holland and George Bevis probably refer to actors who played the parts of these characters and "that Shakespeare used their names . . . for convenience, or through a slip."[2] Saunder, too, as in Saunder Simpcox, could identify the contemporary actor Alexander Cooke.[3] But Shakespeare's usual practice was to tag low-life characters with label names often occupationally oriented (see, for example, the "rude mechanicals" in *A Midsummer Night's Dream*), and to argue lack of imagination or carelessness where there is another more compelling explanation seems unwarranted. Like Holland, Bevis would be calf-meat, an English favorite (see "bull-beeves," *Henry VI, Part 1,* I, ii, 9).[4] Simpcox surely tags the mental equipment of this character.

SAUNDER
SIMPCOX

GEORGE BEVIS

The names George Bevis and Saunder Simpcox are oxymoronic as well. Coupled with their "humble" family names are the English saint's name and the nickname for Alexander. George Bevis may work the other way, too: George is from the Greek for 'farmer,' and Bevis of [South]Hampton was a legendary and enormously popular English hero celebrated for his feats of arms (see *Henry VIII,* I, i, 38). Camden notes in *Remaines*: "Beavis, may seeme probably to be corrupted from the name of the famous *Celtique* King *Bellovesus*" (pp. 45-46). Alexander Iden's name is from history.

IDEN

A Thomas Hornby was a Warwickshire blacksmith.[5] Thomas *Horner,* however, is perhaps an allusion to the famous steward to the Abbot of Glastonbury Cathedral during the reign of Henry VIII.[6] When the Abbot sent the deeds to twelve manorial estates baked in a pie as a bribe to the King, Tom (not Jack as in the rhyme) "stuck in his thumb and pulled out a plum"—the deed to the manor of Mells. In Shakespeare's play, plums figure in the unmasking of Simpcox (II, i, 94-100), and Thomas Horner is a treasonous armorer revealed by his honest apprentice Peter Thump.

HORNER

In response to learning Peter's family name, Salisbury quibbles: "Thump? Then see thou thump thy master well" (II, iii, 84). The tag goes with the percussive nature of Thump's trade (see *Love's Labor's Lost,* III, i, 65), and the name Peter reveals his

PETER THUMP

religious bent: "Drink, and pray for me, I pray you, for I think I have taken my last draught in this world. Here, Robin, and if I die, I give thee my aporn; and, Will, thou shalt have my hammer; and here, Tom, take all the money that I have. O Lord bless me, I pray God, for I am never able to deal with my master, he hath learnt so much fence already" (II, iii, 72-78). When Peter *thumps* Thomas Horner and the master confesses, the apprentice exclaims rapturously: "O God, have I overcome mine enemies in this presence? O Peter, thou has prevail'd in right!" (II, iii, 97-99).

EMMANUEL

The Clerk of Chartam is Emmanuel, Hebrew for "God with us" (Camden's *Remaines,* p. 51). Dick points out, "They use to write it [Emmanuel] on the top of letters" (IV, ii, 100), referring to the practice of prefixing contemporary correspondence with this sort of salutation.

MARGERY JORDAN

Margery Jordan may have a real-life counterpart in the notorious Witch of Eye.[7] Her last name sounds her ominous note: she "deigns the light of day." Witches being expert with plants and such, the herb *marjoram* yields her first.[8] The overtones of *conjure* are to be heard in both Margery and Jordan. Actually, her given

MARGARET

Christian name is Margaret, linking her with Margaret of Anjou, the play's witch-like woman of a higher station.

DE LA POLE

Queen Margaret's lover, de la Pole, has a name with phallic implication, but it is played with also in another sense:

> Poole! Sir Poole! lord!
> Ay, kennel, puddle, sink, whose filth and dirt
> Troubles the silver spring where England drinks.
> Now will I [Lieutenant speaking] dam up this thy yawning
> mouth
> For swallowing the treasure of the realm.   (IV, i, 70-74)

Pole's title is the occasion for word play by York: "For Suffolk's duke, may he be suffocate" (I, i, 124). The prophecy that, "By water shall he die, and take his end" (I, iv, 33), foretells the first name of his

WALTER WHITMORE

assassin Walter (pronounced *water*) Whitmore:

> Thy name affrights me, in whose sound is death.
> A cunning man did calculate my birth

30

And told me that by water I should die:
Yet let not this make thee be bloody-minded;
Thy name is Gualtier, being rightly sounded.

(IV, i, 33-37)

Vaux is the 'voice' announcing Cardinal Beauford's mortal illness (III, ii, 367-379). The Duchess's name Eleanor is negatively toned here, as in *King John* for the character Elinor of Aquitaine.

VAUX

ELEANOR

Henry VI, Part 3

In his discussion of the sources for *Henry VI, Part 3*, Geoffrey Bullough notes that "Most of the names in the play are historical."[9] There is, however, little factual basis for Shakespeare's picture of Bona of Savoy as the projected bride for Edward IV. Yet her name serves him well to point up the 'good' Lady Bona's wronging by the lecherous King Edward. Concerned as it is with episodic historical narrative, the last part of *Henry VI* has no significant name play.

BONA

Richard III

It is consistent that Richard, whose behavior is amorally animal-like and whose crest is a boar, should have among his friends other animals—*Rat*cliffe and *Cat*esby. Shakespeare was undoubtedly familiar with William Collingbourne's couplet, to be found in Holinshed's *Chronicles* among other places: "The catte, the ratte, and Lovell our dogge/ Rulyth all England under a hogge."

Early in the action of *Richard III*, the Duke of Clarence is

RATCLIFFE

CATESBY

GEORGE

committed to the Tower for his name George, which is portentous to his brother King:

> He hearkens after prophecies and dreams,
> And from the cross-row plucks the letter G,
> And says a wizard told him that by G
> His issue disinherited should be;
> And for my name of George begins with G,
> It follows in his thought that I am he.   (I, i, 54-59)

Edward should fear, to be sure, his other brother Richard, Duke of Gloucester, whose *title* begins with the fated letter G.

DIGHTON

FORREST

TYRREL

The off-stage killing of the young princes is accomplished by two historical but nonetheless ominously named murderers, Dighton and Forrest.[10] Dighton suggests 'deal with' or 'put to death' (see *O.E.D., dight*), and Forrest calls up darkness and evil. Tyrrel is also an historical personage, and his name is again connotative. It suggests *tire,* 'to feed or prey ravenously upon,' as a hawk does (see *Henry VI, Part 3,* I, i, 269 and *Venus and Adonis,* l. 56).

TRESSEL

BRAKENBURY

RICHMOND

Although the name Berkeley has no apparent significance, the other "gentleman" attending bereaved Lady Anne is Tressel, and his name could imply a support or prop (*trestle*). A similar tag is Brakenbury (*break* and *bury*), most appropriate for the Lieutenant of the Tower, but not in keeping with Sir Robert's affirmatively drawn character. At the end of the play, Richmond's title carries with it the idea of rich 'world'—the promise of peace after bloody Richard's reign.

King John

For a Shakespeare history play *King John* has a limited *Dramatis Personae,* and virtually all of the names are from historical sources. Even James Gurney, the name of Lady Faulconbridge's servant, which triggers suspicions of deliberateness because apparently it was invented by the playwright, seems without special relevance.

    The only distinctive feature of the nomenclature in the play is the abundance of royal Christian names: John, Henry, Philip, Lewis, Richard, and, to be sure, Arthur. Here is Shakespeare's only use of the highly charged Arthur for a character. The name Philip is used both for the French King and, at first, the Bastard. Although it derives from the Greek word for 'lover of horses' (see Lyford's *The true Interpretation . . . of Christian Names,* p. 149), Philip became associated with sparrows as an approximation of their characteristic peep. The Bastard couples *Philip* and *sparrow* in his following exchange with Gurney:

    Bast. James Gurney, wilt thou give us leave a while?
    Gur. Good leave, good Philip.
    Bast.   Philip? sparrow! James,
    There's toys abroad; anon I'll tell thee more. (I, i, 230-232)

We recall that John Skelton published a "Philip Sparrow" (in 1568), and George Gascoigne also wrote in "Praise of Philip Sparrow."

    With his name change to Richard, in honor of his supposed father Richard Coeur-de-Lion, the Bastard is metamorphosed from sparrow to lion:

    K. John. What is thy name?
    Bast. Philip, my liege, so is my name begun,
    Philip, good old Sir Robert's wive's eldest son.
    K. John. From henceforth bear his name whose
                      form thou bearest:
    Kneel thou down Philip, but rise more great,
    Arise Sir Richard, and Plantagenet.   (I, i, 157-162)

In his soliloquy which follows, the Bastard swaggers with his new found name: "'Good den, Sir Richard!' 'God-a-mercy, fellow!'/ And if his name be George, I'll call him Peter;/ For new-made honor doth forget men's names" (I, i, 185-187). Faulconbridge has noble connotations associated with the bird, a bird appearing on the Shakespeare family coat of arms.

ARTHUR
PHILIP

RICHARD

FAULCONBRIDGE

33

ELINOR
CONSTANCE
BLANCH

Of the women characters, Queen Elinor is negatively drawn like her namesake in *Henry VI, Part 2,* Constance is constant to her son without special mention in the play's dialogue, and Blanch has an innocence consistent with her name.

Richard II

GAUNT

In *Richard II* the sick Gaunt banters with his name:

O how that name befits my composition!
Old Gaunt indeed, and gaunt in being old.
Within me grief hath kept a tedious fast;
And who abstains from meat that is not gaunt?
For sleeping England long time have I watch'd,
Watching breeds leanness, leanness is all gaunt.
The pleasure that some fathers feed upon
Is my strict fast—I mean, my children's looks;
And therein fasting, hast thou made me gaunt.
Gaunt am I for the grave, gaunt as a grave,
Whose hollow womb inherits nought but bones. (II, i, 73-83)

King Richard asks, "Can sick men play so nicely with their names?" (II, i, 84), and Gaunt replies:

No, misery makes sport to mock itself:
Since thou dost seek to kill my name in me,
I mock my name, great King, to flatter thee. (II, i, 85-87)

Gaunt's name stems from his birthplace of Ghent in Flanders.

BULLINGBROOK

So too does Bullingbrook come from a birthplace—Henry's father's Leicestershire castle. In the abdication scene, Richard plays on the name Bullingbrook when he exclaims: "God pardon all oaths that are *broke* to me!/God keep all vows *unbroke* are made to thee!" (italics mine, IV, i, 214-215). That Shakespeare has a conjurer Bolingbrook in *Henry VI, Part 2* might underline Henry's evil usurpation of Richard's crown.

A momentarily manic Richard, returned from Ireland but facing rapidly evaporating support, asks:

> Is not the king's name twenty thousand names?
> Arm, arm, my name! a puny subject strikes
> At thy great glory.   (III, ii, 85-87)

But Richard "Must . . . lose/ The name of king, a' God's name" (III, iii, 145-146), and be "lesser than . . . [his] name" (III, iii, 137) because of Bullingbrook's power. Richard must at last come to realize: "I have no name, no title,/ No, not that name was given me at the font" (IV, i, 255-256).

The King's friends, Bushy, Bagot, Green, and Wiltshire (II, i, 215; III, ii, 122), suggest an uncared for garden with their names; the Queen's scene with Bushy and Bagot at II, ii previews the allegorical garden scene later on (III, iv). To Henry,

BUSHY
BAGOT
GREEN
WILTSHIRE

> . . . Bushy, Bagot, and their complices [are]
> The caterpillars of the commonwealth, [and]
> . . . I have sworn to weed and pluck [them] away.
>   (II, iii, 165-167)

Later, the Gardener confirms Henry's ultimate success when he says:

> The weeds . . .
> Are pluck'd up root and all by Bullingbrook,
> I mean the Earl of Wiltshire, Bushy, Green. (III, iv, 50-53)

Appearing in the last scenes of the play, Richard's own executioner has the tag Sir Pierce of Exton. His name looks ahead to Falstaff's witty quibble, in the first part of *Henry IV*, on Hotspur's family name: "if Percy be alive, I'll pierce him" (V, iii, 56).

PIERCE

Henry IV, Part 1

HOTSPUR

Many characters have meaningful names in the two parts of *Henry IV*. This would be expected because Shakespeare invented non-historical low-life actions in the plays. Yet even some of the nobles' names inherited from sources are significant for the playwright. Hotspur's is the most obvious. Shakespeare created an impulsive, impetuous, and choleric personality to go with the name he read in Holinshed's *Chronicles*.

HAL

FALSTAFF

Shakespeare juxtaposes the two Harrys by using their alliterative nicknames, Hotspur and Hal. Hal comes from the Old English *haele* for 'hero.' Hotspur conveys phallic potency and contrasts meaningfully with the name Falstaff, implying "fallen staff" for impotence. The spur and the sword are traditional symbols of masculinity, just as the distaff (used in spinning) is a female insignia. With the character Falstaff in mind, we recall the Porter's astute observations on drink and lechery in *Macbeth:*

> Lechery, sir, it [drink] provokes, and unprovokes: it provokes the desire, but it takes away the performance. Therefore much drink may be said to be an equivocator with lechery: it makes him, and it mars him; it sets him on, and it takes him off; it persuades him, and disheartens him; makes him stand to, and not stand to; in conclusion, equivocates him in a sleep, and giving him the lie, leaves him.
>
> (II, iii, 29-36)

Hotspur's rough but engaging masculinity is underlined by the bawdy and affectionate scene with his wife Kate (III, i, 226-262).

KATHERINE

Katherine is one of Shakespeare's favorite female names, as evidenced by the numerous Kates in the plays. For Hotspur's wife, the playwright bent the historical Eleanor, which Holinshed misreported as Elizabeth. We recall that Eleanor (with its various spellings) was a name Shakespeare associated with unattractive women in his earlier history plays.

OWEN GLENDOWER

As with Hotspur, Shakespeare read "Owen Glendower" in the *Chronicles* and the name drew forth the character. The deep vowels of both Owen and Glendower ring ominous and other-worldly, just right for the superstitious but compelling personality of Shakespeare's Welshman. The last name denotes a dour glen, mysterious and foreboding. The first is from the Old Welsh *owein,* 'well born,' or 'warrior.'

The Earl of Douglas is "brave Archibald,/ That ever-valiant and approved Scot" (I, i, 53-54). Archibald is a name made up of two words of Germanic origin, *ercan,* 'simple,' and *bald,* 'bold.' Yet another name from history which seems a tag for the character the playwright invents is Sir Walter Blunt. Blunt is forthright in delivering the King's message to the rebels. After a few personal remarks, he stops himself: "But to my charge" (IV, iii, 41). Blunt's response to Hotspur's verbal evasion is: "Tut, I came not to hear this" (IV, iii, 89). The character is also forthright when facing Archibald in battle (V, iii).

ARCHIBALD

BLUNT

The name change from Sir John Oldcastle to Sir John Falstaff is too well-known to repeat in detail here.[11] The earlier name was a cant term for roisterer, and it may also have suggested to Shakespeare the idea of decadent aristocracy or fallen knighthood—the "old castle" nobility in ruin. The Prince calls Falstaff, "my old lad of the castle" (I, ii, 41-42), a play on the original name. When Shakespeare changed the name Oldcastle to Falstaff, he must have remembered his earlier character in *Henry VI, Part 1,* who ran from battle.

OLDCASTLE

The various spellings of *Falstaff* are interchangeable, but one or another can provide a clue to contemporary pronunciation. For example, the 1598 *Stationer's Register* entry "ffalstoff" suggests something akin to *full stuff,* apt for the fat knight who is *full of stuff* and, at times, a *stuffed fool.* The word *fat* can be spelled forward and backward in the name's usual spelling. Falstaff also yields *false staff*—that is, faulty prop or inadequate support for the soon-to-be ruler. A staff of stewardship is referred to at V, i, 34, and in *Henry VI, Part 3,* Edward complains that York, his former "prop to lean upon," now that he is gone "we have no staff, no stay" (II, i, 68-69). In *Antony and Cleopatra,* the young conqueror Caesar offers the defeated Cleopatra "a staff/ To lean upon" (III, xiii, 68-69).

FALSTAFF

Falstaff's associates also have meaningful names, and most of them are tags of sorts. Gadshill has his name from the notorious place of highway robbery, Gads Hill, on the road between

GADSHILL

PETO London and Canterbury. Peto refers to *pétard,* a 'small weapon' (see *Hamlet,* III, iv, 207), but slang for 'penis.' In Latin, *peto* means 'I attack, assail,' etc. The name additionally suggests the French *pétard* for 'break wind.'

QUICKLY Since Mistress Quickly is or has been a bawd, the last syllable of her name has an obvious connotation.[12] The surname as a whole indicates the bustle and energy of the character. Poins is

POINS presumably as tiny and insignificant as a point.

Henry IV, Part 2

Some of the same actors to be found in *Henry IV, Part 1* are continued in *Part 2,* but this second part shows a proliferation of characters, especially for the comic sub-plot. Of the nobles met before, we learn with Northumberland that at Shrewsbury "young Harry Percy's spur was cold" (I, i, 42). The Earl picks up the play on his son's name: "Said he young Harry Percy's spur was cold?/ Of Hotspur, Coldspur?" (I, i, 49-50).

TRAVERS The newly introduced Travers, who brings news of Hotspur's defeat in the first scene of the play, is an appropriate messenger; his name in Old French means 'from the crossroads.'

HARCOURT Harcourt, deriving as it does from Old Franco-German *hari-court,* 'from the fortified castle,' seems apt for an officer in Henry's army.

MORTON Hotspur's death is reported by Morton (I, i, 105-111), whose tidings mortally wound the better news brought by Lord

BARDOLPH Bardolph. Why there should be two Bardolphs in this play may be a consequence of Shakespeare's changing the Lord's name from Harvey during revision.[13] The playwright may have known an actual Bardolph, as there is a George Bardolfe who, together with one William Fluellen, appears on a 1592 recusancy list for Stratford, a list which includes as well the name of Shakespeare's father. In any case, Florio hints at a way to play the lord, giving the following translation of the word *bardo:* "blunt or blockish."

38

Mistress Quickly appears to have acquired the first name Ursula in this play, ironic for her in that Ursula was a maiden saint.[14] She wishes Falstaff for her husband, but it is the Ancient Pistol she marries. His name ignites some witty play:

> *Fal.* Welcome, Ancient Pistol. Here, Pistol, I charge you with a cup of sack, do you discharge upon mine hostess.
> *Pist.* I will discharge upon her, Sir John, with two bullets.
> *Fal.* She is pistol-proof, sir; you shall not hardly offend her.
> *Host.* Come, I'll drink no proofs nor no bullets. I'll drink no more than will do me good, for no man's pleasure, I.
> . . .
> *Fal.* No more, Pistol, I would not have you go off here. Discharge yourself of our company, Pistol. (II, iv, 111-137)

The Hostess makes the bawdy quibbling even clearer when she refers to her husband as "Good Captain Peesel" (II, iv, 161). Pistol's explosive personality is remarked by the King in *Henry V*: the name Pistol "sorts well with your fierceness" (IV, i, 63). The Renaissance pistol was rather unreliable and noisy too.[15]

Justice Shallow wants intellectual depth. His friend's name prompts the following witty comment from Falstaff: "Good Master Silence, it well befits you should be of the peace" (III, ii, 89-90). But Silence is not always so, a Justice of the Peace, as his lusty singing at V, iii attests. Fang means 'capture or catch,' and the character instructs his "yeoman," "Snare, we must arrest Sir John Falstaff" (II, i, 8). "Good Master Fang, hold him sure. Good Master Snare, let him not scape" (II, i, 24-26), worries the Hostess, underlining the tags.

Falstaff has great fun playing with the names of the motley group of country recruits. Says Falstaff of Mouldy, "'Tis the more time thou wert us'd" (III, ii, 106), the joke in which Justice Shallow pedantically explains: "Things that are mouldy lack use" (III, ii, 107-108). But not to be outdone, Falstaff has the last word: "Mouldy, it is time you were spent" (III, ii, 116-117). Shadow's name indicates his physique and provides occasion for some son-sun punning. When Falstaff is told that Shadow is his "mother's son," he responds: "Thy mother's son! like enough, and thy father's shadow.

So the son of the female is the shadow of the male. It is often so indeed, but much of the father's substance" (III, ii, 128-131). Fictitious names placed on contemporary muster-rolls to draw extra pay for unscrupulous captains were referred to as *shadows*, as we learn from Falstaff's comment: "Shadow will serve for summer, prick him, [*aside*] for we have a number of shadows fill up the muster-book" (III, ii, 133-135). Thomas is "a very ragged [hairy]" Wart (III, ii, 141). Feeble and Bullcalf are obvious tags.

WART

FEEBLE

BULLCALF

DOLL TEARSHEET

      Both of Doll Tearsheet's names identify her as a prostitute. Coleridge's embarrassed attempt to make her a "Tear*street*," and thus more respectable, has never inspired much agreement.[16] Jane Nightwork is similarly tagged for her occupation (III, ii, 198-199). Sneak is a musician with no lines, but a name indicating his furtive actions (II, iv, 11). Most of the persons mentioned in the dialogue have lively denotative names: Samson Stockfish (III, ii, 32), Master Tisick (consumptive cough) (II, iv, 85), Master Dumbe (II, iv, 88), Goodwife Keech (animal fat for tallow) (II, i, 93), Master Dommelton (blockhead) (I, ii, 29), Master Smooth ("the silk-man") (II, i, 29), Master Surecard (III, ii, 86). "John Doit of Staffordshire, and black George Barnes, and Francis Pickbone, and Will Squele, a Cotsole man" (III, ii, 19-21) have colorful names that sound as if they might have belonged to actual people.

NIGHTWORK

SNEAK

STOCKFISH

TISICK

DUMBE

KEECH

DOMMELTON

SMOOTH

SURECARD

Henry V

With its emphasis on patriotic historical themes and the glorification of King Henry as an epic hero, the purposes of *Henry V* are alien to elaborate name signification. Yet Shakespeare is nonetheless deliberate about some of his naming in the play. Fluellen has a Welsh name, MacMorris is Irish, and Jamy obviously Scottish; here is Britain in miniature. John Bates, Alexander Court, and Michael Williams all have popular English names, with Alexander and Michael further reminding us of famous warriors. The King moves

FLUELLEN

MacMORRIS

JAMY

BATES

ALEXANDER COURT

MICHAEL WILLIAMS

40

among his troops with the alias Harry le Roy, which Pistol mistakenly thinks "a Cornish name" (IV, i, 49), but which means, to be sure, 'Henry the King.'

HARRY LE ROY

Princess Katherine of France is another of Shakespeare's engaging Kates. It is appropriate that her attending lady Alice should have a name with Old French roots (*Aliz, Asliz, Adaliz*).

KATHERINE
ALICE

Of the comic characters, only Nym we have not met before. His name, from the word *nim*, is a synonym for 'filch, steal, or pilfer.' In the play, he is reported as ultimately hanged together with Bardolph for looting French churches (IV, iv, 70-74). Now married to Pistol, Mistress Quickly has acquired the nickname Nell for this play (see II, i, 18).

NYM

NELL

Henry VIII

The Duke of Buckingham remarks his reduction of name to "poor Edward Bohun" (II, i, 103), and this seems the only male name in *Henry VIII* underlined by Shakespeare. However, both the playwright and his audience would have been aware that Anne Bullen's Christian name is the same as that of Saint Ann, mother of the Virgin in the apocryphal gospels. Thus, Anne's child Elizabeth is identified as the Virgin Queen. Further, the play itself may have been written for the marriage festivities of Elizabeth, daughter of James I and Queen Anne, these names thus suggesting additionally contemporary reference.[17]

ANNE

ELIZABETH

Saint Catherine, too, is invoked by way of the noble Katherine in the play. The spiked wheel associated with this saint's martyrdom, known as a "Catherine Wheel," picks up the Wheel of Fortune motif, one of the strongest in *Henry VIII*. Katherine derives from *katharos*, the Greek word for 'pure,' as the wronged Queen surely is. Her attendant Patience, a character Shakespeare invents, reinforces with her name the Queen's nobility as she awaits death.[18]

KATHERINE

PATIENCE

$$3 \quad \text{TRAGEDIES}$$

The popular titles of all of Shakespeare's tragedies—*Titus Andronicus* to *Timon of Athens*—are from character names. Except for *Julius Caesar,* each title points to the play's tragic hero or paired lovers. The tragedies also have in them significant *unnamed* characters: the fool in *King Lear,* the grave-digger in *Hamlet,* the porter in *Macbeth.* Consistent with the tragic genre's emphasis on concentrated action to produce heightened emotion, these plays have the fewest named characters. In general, the Roman plays tend to be the most expansive. Like Shakespeare's plays of English history, the tragedies are also "historical" and many character names derive from sources.

Titus Andronicus

Plutarch's "Life of Scipio Africanus" gives Shakespeare the names for half of his twenty named characters in *Titus Andronicus*: Titus, Marcus, Martius, Quintus, Lucius (old and young), Caius, Aemilius, Publius, and Sempronius.[1] The title character's name derives from the Greek word for 'giant' (see *Genesis* 6:4), and the mythic Titans who battled Zeus. Edward Lyford's 1655 name dictionary lists Titus as meaning "Defender, ... honored, esteemed" (p. 178). In a play with rape at its center, the King of the Sabines, Titus Tatius, who warred against Rome after the rape of his women, may also have been in Shakespeare's mind. Andronicus, says Lyford, is "a man of victory" (p. 24). Although the historical emperor Andronicus Comnenus (1183-1185) shares Titus' family name and was mutilated by having his hand cut off, he was noted for cruelty and does not seem to be the model for Shakespeare's hero.[2] Another Andronicus was a Roman dramatic and epic poet of the third century B.C. Why Titus should additionally be "surnamed Pius" (I,i,23) is puzzling, despite the 'dutiful,' 'patriotic,' 'devoted,' 'honest,' and 'upright' character the supernumerary implies.

TITUS

ANDRONICUS

Brother Marcus is named for a warrior, although he is the milder Andronicus. Both he and Titus' son Martius have names derived from Mars, the Roman war god. Quintus denotes 'fifth child' in a play where the number of Titus' sons is stressed.

MARCUS
MARTIUS
QUINTUS

Lucius suggests light (from the Latin *lucius,* 'born during the day'), appropriate for the character who ultimately restores order and rules Rome at the end of the play. Young Lucius' name implies the continuance of this rule for the next generation (see V, iii, 160-175). Shakespeare was inordinately fond of *Luc-* names. There are characters with this first syllable in their name in no less than eight plays ranging throughout his career.

LUCIUS

Aemilius, Sempronius, and Caius are noble Roman names. Aemilius comes from the Latin for 'flattering one,' apt for a court functionary. Sempronius suggests faithfulness (from the Latin *semper,* 'always'). Caius will be the noble Roman alias Kent chooses in the later *King Lear.* Publius, son of the people's tribune Marcus Andronicus, is also 'of the people.'

AEMILIUS
SEMPRONIUS
CAIUS

PUBLIUS

What of the names not to be found in the "Life of Scipio Africanus?" Perhaps Marcus and Martius put the planets in Shakespeare's mind. The references to heavenly bodies and the comic episode with the Clown and "Jupiter" (IV,iii) go with the name Saturninus. Presumably the character was born under Saturn and is therefore 'morose, of a sluggish, cold, and gloomy temperament' (see *Much Ado About Nothing,* I,iii,10-11).

SATURNINUS

BASSIANUS

Bassianus might derive from the Latin *basium* for 'a kiss.' The name looks forward to another of Shakespeare's romantic heroes, Bassanio, in *The Merchant of Venice*. Titus' mutinous son

MUTIUS

Mutius has a name appropriate to his rebellion in the play's first

VALENTINE

scene. Valentine shoots arrows—of course.

DEMETRIUS

The name Demetrius suggests the lust of the character with its derivation from the fertility goddess Demeter (see Lyford, p. 48). The Latin *demeto* means 'mow, reap, cut down.' Such meaning is driven home with Demetrius' sadistic line after killing Bassianus and intending to rape Lavinia: "First thrash the corn, then after burn

CHIRON

the straw" (II,iii,123). Brother Chiron has his name from Charon, ferryman of the underworld, not from Chiron, a "good" centaur in Ovid (*Metamorphoses* II,236). The first syllable of the name would be pronounced "cur" to indicate his animal nature.[3]

TAMORA

May Tamora's name allude to Tomyris, the Scythian queen mentioned in *Henry VI, Part 1* (II,iii,6), who avenged her son's death by killing Cyrus the Great and preserving his head in a blood-filled wineskin? The biblical Tamar might also be a source. After discarding Semiramis as not "barbarous" enough, Lavinia observes to Tamora, "no name fits thy nature but thy own" (II,iii,119).

LAVINIA

Lavinia's namesake is to be found in the last six books of Virgil's *Aeneid*.[4] Despite a previous betrothal, she is promised to Aeneas by her father, and thus becomes the innocent cause of much anguish. As the daughter of Latinus, Lavinia is a symbol for Rome as in Shakespeare's play.[5] In the play, she is "Gracious Lavinia, Rome's rich ornament" (I, i, 52). The "vinia" in her name could suggest 'wine,' because of her father's reference to her as "The cordial of mine age" (I, i, 166).

AARON

As noted above, Tamora may allude to a biblical figure; Aaron does without question (see *Exodus* 32). Aaron, we recall, was Moses' brother who fashioned the golden calf. Salted throughout Aaron's first soliloquy (II, i, 1-24), and in other places as well, are references to gold: he buries gold under a tree (II, iii, 1-8). With his Hebrew name, as well as with his black color, Aaron stands out as foreign and alien.

A final note on the poetic use of names in *Titus Andronicus*. Shakespeare juxtaposes a name with a similar sounding word four times in the play: "Tamora./ To-morrow" (I, i, 491-492);

44

"Lavinia, live" (I, i, 167); "Lavinia lives" (III, i, 294); and "Mark, Marcus, mark!" (III, i, 143). He also juxtaposes characters by using the sound of names. Titus and Tamora are foils and their names alliterate, as do Andronicus and Aaron. Moor is to be noticed within Tamora's name, and the characters Tamora and Aaron are lovers. The endings of Tamora and Lavinia sound similar for these two women antagonists. Titus and Marcus jingle together, and the characters are brothers. So, too, are Saturninus and Bassianus.

Romeo and Juliet

In *Romeo and Juliet,* Harry Levin notes, "Shakespeare balances the rival claims with symmetry and objectivity by making them metrically equivalent: *Montague/Capulet, Romeo Montague/ Juliet Capulet.*"[6] There is also to be observed the harmony of sound resulting from the common 'o' ending of the friends' names: Romeo, Mercutio, Benvolio. This harmony is set against the cacophonous clash of Tybalt and Paris, the names of the outsiders.

MONTAGUE

Montague is a name that came to England as early as the Norman Conquest (meaning 'dweller at the pointed hill'), and it is a corruption of the Veronese family name Montecchi.[7] Montague seems covertly masculine, with its faint echo of "mounting," and thus apt for the lover Romeo. Florio lists *montare,* "to mount, to ascende, to climbe, etc." Capulet, on the other hand, has feminine connotations, suggesting as it does "capitulating," giving in. The Latin *capulus* is 'coffin.' Both the chaste Diana and her widowed mother in *All's Well That Ends Well* are other female Capilets (though with a different spelling), as is "grey Capilet," Sir Andrew Aguecheek's horse in *Twelfth Night.* Sir Andrew is a ludicrous lover, and a horse is all the lady he deserves; the *O.E.D.* lists *capel* for 'horse.' Capuletti was the original Italian version of the name.

CAPULET

Juliet's Christian name is derived from her birth month; the Nurse tells us that she was born on "Lammas-eve at night" (I, iii,

JULIET

17), July 31. Her name looks forward to Julius, the Caesar who gives his name to Shakespeare's next tragedy. The playwright also uses Juliet for Claudio's betrothed in *Measure for Measure,* and the similar Julia for Proteus' fiancée in *The Two Gentlemen of Verona.*

ROMEO

Although Juliet's feelings on the subject of Romeo's name vary wildly, in one place she says, "every tongue that speaks/ But Romeo's name speaks heavenly eloquence" (III, ii, 32-33). The Nurse too likes Romeo, "Doth not rosemary and Romeo begin both with a letter?" (II, iv, 206-207); perhaps she remembers that rosemary goes with weddings (see S.D. IV, v, 95-96). The witty Mercutio finds in Romeo the occasion for a pun, when the character shows up at one point "Without his roe [looking thin], like a dried herring" (II, iv, 37). But Romeo deplores his own name. In response to the Nurse's description of Juliet crying over Tybalt and invoking her lover, Romeo curses:

> As if that name,
> Shot from the deadly level of a gun,
> Did murther her, as that name's cursed hand
> Murder'd her kinsman. (III, iii, 102-105)

He appeals to the friar:

> O, tell me, friar, tell me,
> In what vile part of this anatomy
> Doth my name lodge? Tell me, that I may sack
> The hateful mansion. (III, iii, 105-108)

Yet Romeo's name is most apt for Shakespeare's play. Knight observes justly that it "contains a handsome set of hints: the nobility of 'Rome' or 'Roman', the *romantic* connotations of 'rom-'; a sturdy suggestion of 'roaming' . . . ; and yet, since it is a lover, a lighter, falling, quality in the penultimate 'e', countered by a strong rise on the final 'o'. It is a suitable name for a sturdy young man whose role is that of a lover, and, despite Juliet's argument, it is necessary. Shakespeare was right to accept it without further question."[8] Florio has the following after *Roméo*: "a roamer, a wandrer, a palmer."

Mercutio is similarly fortuitous. The Roman god Mercury

was, among other things, a god of oratory and eloquence. Mercutio is
characterized by Romeo as "A gentleman . . . that loves to hear
himself talk, and will speak more in a minute than he will stand to in
a month" (II, iv, 147-149). At the close of *Love's Labor's Lost*
Shakespeare warns, however, that "The words of Mercury are
harsh" (V, ii, 930). Shakespeare's volatile, impulsive, "mercurial"
character, full of inspired "words," is created from merely one
mention in Arthur Brooke's source poem. A name not to be found in
The Tragical History of Romeus and Juliet is Benvolio, 'good will' in
Shakespeare's Italian, an apt label for Mercutio's peaceful counter.
One inevitably thinks of Malvolio from *Twelfth Night* who has this
same sort of tag name.

    Tybalt's is an allusive name, recalling the cat in the
medieval history of *Reynard the Fox*. The sharp-tongued Mercutio
calls Tybalt "rat-catcher" (III, i, 75), "Prince of Cats" (II, iv, 19), and
"King of Cats" (III, i, 77), and refers to his own death wound as a
"scratch" (III, i, 93, 101) to underline the allusion. The mythical Paris
associates Shakespeare's County with a lover, and the famous
Judgment is perhaps also recalled with Escalus, which is from the
Italian *della scala*, 'of the scales,' 'justice.' The Prince of Verona
renders decisions at "old Free-town, our common judgment-place"
(I, i, 102). There is a humane old counselor Escalus in *Measure for
Measure*.

    Both Friars, Lawrence and John, have religiously allusive
names of saints. The Capulet servants' names are biblical, one with
Old Testament associations, the other with New—Sampson and
Gregory. The Montague servants' names balance neatly—Abram
and Balthasar. Peter is also biblical, but it is additionally an appropriately bawdy name for the Nurse's "man." Says Peter ambiguously to
his mistress: "I saw no man use you at his pleasure; if I had, my
weapon should quickly have been out. I warrant you, I dare draw as
soon as another man, if I see occasion in a good quarrel, and the law
on my side" (II, iv, 157-160). Apparently the Nurse herself is named
"Angelica" (IV, iv, 5), and she is also, continuing the irony, "Lady
Wisdom" and "Good Prudence" (III, v, 170-171) to old Capulet. The
rose Rosaline does not smell so sweet to Romeo after he meets his
true love: "I have forgot that name, and that name's woe" (II, iii, 46).

    The nameless servant of Act I cannot read his list of

MERCUTIO

BENVOLIO

TYBALT

PARIS

ESCALUS

LAWRENCE
JOHN
SAMPSON
GREGORY
ABRAM
BALTHASAR
PETER

ANGELICA

ROSALINE

colorful Italian names to be invited to the Capulet party, and gets Romeo to help him: "Signior Martino," "County Anselme," "the lady widow of [Vitruvio]," "Signior Placentio," "Valentine," "Livia," "Signior Valentio," "Lucio," and "Helena" (I, ii, 64-70) are mixed with the names of characters we know already. Together with "The son and heir of old Tiberio" (I, v, 129) and the "young Petruchio" (I, v, 131) at the ball, the names spice the Italian flavor of the Verona setting.

CATLING
REBECK
SOUNDPOST
POTPAN
GRINDSTONE

Finally, the musicians have names that go with their profession. Simon Catling takes his from a catgut fiddle string (see *Troilus and Cressida,* III, iii, 304). Hugh Rebeck's is from the three-stringed fiddle itself, which would have a "Soundpost" as in James, the other member of the Trio. Potpan and Susan Grindstone work in the kitchen (I, v, 9-10).

Julius Caesar

CINNA

Shakespeare's hand on the names in *Julius Caesar* is light, perhaps because of the familiar historical subject matter. Even the episode where the poet Cinna is dragged off by the mob to be killed, because he happens to have the same name as one of the conspirators (III, iii), is not Shakespeare's own; he found it repeated in both Plutarch's "Life of Caesar" and "Life of Brutus."

BRUTUS

The playwright probably was aware of and playing with the Latin meanings of *brutus*—'heavy, immovable, dull, without feeling or reason'—when he has Brutus characterize himself as follows: "I am not gamesome; I do lack some part/ Of that quick spirit that is in Antony" (I, ii, 28-29). The lines of Antony's famous speech, "O judgment! thou [art] fled to brutish beasts,/ And men have lost their reason" (III, ii, 104-105), seems a play on these meanings as well.[9] The quibble is surely intentional in Shakespeare's next tragedy when Hamlet says of Brutus: "It was a brute part of him to kill so capital a calf" (III, ii, 105-106). Brutus' so-called "mis-

48

takes"—allowing Antony to live, and to speak his eulogy last—may be seen as a part of the 'dullness' implied by his name.

Cassius tempts Brutus to the murder of Caesar with reference to their names:

> Brutus and Caesar: what should be in that "Caesar"?
> Why should that name be sounded more than yours?
> Write them together, yours is as fair a name;
> Sound them, it doth become the mouth as well;
> Weigh them, it is as heavy; conjure with 'em,
> "Brutus" will start a spirit as soon as "Caesar." (I, ii, 142-147)

Cassius' own name may come from the Latin *cassus* to suggest 'empty, hollow, worthless, useless, or vain.'

In *Titus Andronicus* we noted that Marcus derives from the god Mars. Here Brutus has the name, Antony a variant, Lepidus an initial standing for it, and Cicero lacks it despite it belonging to his historical counterpart. The Latin *Antonius* in its Italian form *Antonio* is used often by Shakespeare for characters in his comedies. And *Luc-* syllable names are also favorites of the playwright. In *Julius Caesar* we have Lucilius and Lucius. Lucius—'light'—is called for his master to provide candles (II, i, 7).

Antony carefully names each name of each conspirator as he shakes their hands:

> Let each man render me his bloody hand.
> First, Marcus Brutus, will I shake with you;
> Next, Caius Cassius, do I take your hand;
> Now, Decius Brutus, yours; now yours, Metellus;
> Yours, Cinna; and, my valiant Casca, yours;
> Though last, not least in love, yours, good Trebonius.
>
> (III, i, 184-189)

He does this to single out the men as individual murderers. Afterwards, he asks pardon of his friend's corpse, familiarly calling it "Julius" to emphasize his love (III, i, 204).

Immediately following the assassination, the Roman Senator Publius becomes a symbol for all the 'people.' Brutus greets

CASSIUS

MARCUS
ANTONY

LUCILIUS
LUCIUS

PUBLIUS

49

him: "Publius, good cheer,/ There is no harm intended to your person,/ Nor to no Roman else. So tell them, Publius" (III, i, 89-91). Metellus Cimber's banished brother is another Publius (III, i, 53) and has a name not to be found in Plutarch. Yet another Publius is Antony's nephew to be killed (IV, i, 4). The "people" are so easily

POPILIUS LENA   manipulated by their leaders. Popilius Lena's name suggests the populous he represents. Lena is derived from the Latin for 'bawd'— an interesting tag for a politican.

Hamlet

Name origins are especially varied in *Hamlet,* deriving from languages as different as Latin, Italian, French, German, and Icelandic. Shakespeare's intention is to suggest with his names universality for his drama: Denmark is a microcosm for the world.

HAMLET   Hamlet's own name is ironic—it comes from the Icelandic word for "simpleton."[10] Thus, he seems named in the manner of Shakespeare's "brute" Brutus. But "Hamlet" is also properly English, deriving from Norman diminutives of *hamon.*[11] Ruskin found in it the suggestion of " 'homely,' the entire event of the tragedy turning on betrayal of home duty." Perhaps he had in mind the Old Franco-German *hamo-elet* for 'little home.' In the name might be also a pointing up of Hamlet's inability to act: *hame* is Middle English for 'yoke,' and *let* is to 'hinder or prevent,' as in the tennis term.

Hamlet iterates his name in an interesting way when excusing his past actions to Laertes late in the play:

> Was't Hamlet wrong'd Laertes? Never Hamlet!
> If Hamlet from himself be ta'en away,
> And when he's not himself does wrong Laertes,
> Then Hamlet does it not, Hamlet denies it.
> Who does it then? His madness. If't be so,

> Hamlet is of the faction that is wronged,
> His madness is poor Hamlet's enemy.   (V, ii, 233-239)

He identifies his name with the essential part of himself. Shakespeare's only son was named Hamnet, after Hamnet or Hamlet (the spellings are interchangeable) Sadler, mentioned in and a witness to the poet's will.[12] Added to this biographical detail is a curious historical footnote. It seems that one Katherine Hamlet, from a small town near Stratford, drowned herself in the Avon on December 17, 1579.[13] At the inquest which followed, the Stratford town clerk declared her death accidental rather than a suicide. Remarkable echoes of Ophelia. And recall, Katherine was one of Shakespeare's favorite female Christian names, occurring for characters in *The Taming of the Shrew, Love's Labor's Lost, Henry IV, Part 1, Henry V,* and *Henry VIII.*

There are two erring lovers Claudio in Shakespeare, one in *Measure for Measure,* the other in *Much Ado About Nothing.* Their spiritual lameness, as King Claudius' in *Hamlet,* is pointed up with the Latin word in their name: *claudus,* 'lame.' The historical Claudius was, to be sure, a famous Roman Emperor, and the name thus has connotations of nobility as well. Why Shakespeare even mentions a once referred to minor middle-man, Claudio (IV, vii, 40), is puzzling. The reference probably remains from an earlier version of the play.

CLAUDIUS

Polonius is Corambis in the first Quarto edition of *Hamlet.* This name is especially apropos for Shakespeare's character, as it denotes 'tedious iteration' and underscores the old advisor's garrulous comic personality.[14] Yet Polonius too is apt. It suggests the *politic* nature of the counselor, and with its echo reminds that the Polish question is a background for the action. The latinate ending of Polonius allows a certain dignity to the name.

POLONIUS

The Latin Horatius, however, is modified to Horatio, the Italian form, for Shakespeare's character who claims nonetheless he is "more an antique Roman than a Dane" (V, ii, 341). Horatio has the Latin to speak with the Ghost early in the play, and remains to tell the tragic tale at the end. His name recalls the poet Horace.

HORATIO

Laertes and Ophelia both are Greek names. In the myths, Laertes is Ulysses' father, so mentioned in *Titus Andronicus* (I, i,

LAERTES

380). At his first appearance in the play, the King repeats "Laertes" to fix it with the audience:

> And now, Laertes, what's the news with you?
> You told us of some suit, what is't, Laertes,
> You cannot speak of reason to the Dane
> And lose your voice. What wouldst thou beg, Laertes,
> That shall not be my offer, not thy asking?
> . . .
> What wouldst thou have, Laertes?   (I, ii, 42-50)

Perhaps Shakespeare associated the name with a flamboyant character, as the spelling *Leartes* in the first Quarto's stage directions reminds us of an older man of action from a later tragedy. Cordelia and Ophelia seem related names, too.

OPHELIA

Ruskin took Ophelia's name to mean "serviceableness." The Greek *ophéleia* for 'use, help, support' is perhaps the word he had in mind. In Ophelia we hear also *ophis*, 'serpent,' explaining not her evil but the taint of circumstance.

ROSENCRANTZ
GUILDENSTERN

Rosencrantz and Guildenstern are from the Dutch-German: literally, 'garland of roses' and 'golden star.' Although of religious origin, both names together sound sing-song and odd to English ears. Their jingling gives them a lightness, and blurs the individuality of the characters they label.

GERTRUDE

Gertrude is another German name, recalling a mythical Valkyrie.

OSRIC
MARCELLUS
BARNARDO

The Old English *os-ric* translates as 'divine ruler,' an ironic tag for the flamboyant fop. Marcellus and Barnardo are officers with military names in keeping with their profession. The Latin Marcellus, a diminutive of Marcus, is ultimately from Mars. Barnardo designates a courageous soldier, coming from the Old English *beorn* for 'brave or noble.'

FRANCISCO

Francisco in its various forms seems an all purpose name for Shakespeare: characters with it range from the Friar in *Much Ado About Nothing* to the Drawer in *Henry IV, Part 1*.

REYNALDO

Sly Reynard the Fox in the medieval tale gives Reynaldo his name. The sum of Polonius' advice to this "spy" is "By indirections find directions out" (II, i, 63).

FORTINBRAS

Fortinbras in French means 'strong of arm,' apt for a young soldier. Referred to at IV, vii, 92,

52

Lamord sounds like the French *la mort* for 'the death.' Significantly this person is invoked by the King to flatter Laertes into his fatal duel with Hamlet near the end of the play.

And what of Yorick? *George,* surely—a phonetic spelling of the Danish pronunciation. The Greek root of the name suggests that the character is appropriately 'an earthworker.' "Goodman delver" (V, i, 14) is either a tag for one of the grave-diggers or a humorous jibe.

Othello

There are only eleven named characters in *Othello.* The Italian background to the play results in all of the male character names ending in 'o': Brabantio, Gratiano, Lodovico, Othello, Cassio, Iago, Roderigo, and Montano. The only exception is the curious "shadow" Marcus Luccicos, referred to once (I,iii,44); but the other "shadow," Signior Angelo (I,iii,16), has the final 'o' to his name. The three female character names end in 'a': Desdemona, Emilia, and Bianca. These deep vowels in the names of the *Dramatis Personae* sound the tragic music for the play.

Although "the Moor" is spoken about repeatedly from the drama's beginning, Othello's name is not actually mentioned until the third scene. This mention of "Othello" after a suspenseful suspension, as well as the context of its first use, adds muscle to the name: "Valiant Othello, we must straight employ you/ Against the general enemy Ottoman" (I,iii,48-49). The initial and final 'o' in "Othello" ring nobly against the double 'o' in "Ottoman." F. N. Lees thinks that Othoman, the founder of the Ottoman empire, gives Shakespeare the first syllable of his hero's name.[15] Further, "If, as can hardly be avoided, 'Othello' is seen as 'Oth-ello' then we have a familiar Italian diminutive attached to a stem."[16] Shakespeare apparently invented the name Othello, as it does not appear in any of his known sources. Another Shakespearean black man, the Prince of Morocco in *The Merchant of Venice,* has a title with a preponderance of 'o's. Perhaps the occurrence of this vowel in the word *moor* suggested its appropriateness for names of dark-complex-ioned characters: Aaron and Cleopatra also have 'o's in their names.

Ruskin thought Othello meant "the careful," but he does not explain his etymology. Desdemona he translates from the Greek as "miserable fortune." Apparently with "less Greek," in 1710 Shaftesbury asks, "why, amongst his *Greek* names, he shou'd have chosen one which denoted the Lady *Superstitious,* I can't imagine."[17] We read "demon" in the middle of Desdemona's name. In Othello's we read "hell," remembering from *Love's Labor's Lost* that "Black is the badge of hell,/ The hue of dungeons, and the school of night" (IV,iii,250-251).

Iago Ruskin takes to be probably from Jacob, 'the supplanter.' Iago is Spanish for James. Santiago, Saint James, the patron of Spain, was intoned in a national war cry heard by English sailors when fighting the Armada. The shrine to Saint James the Great, called Santiago de Compostelo (Saint James of the Field of the Star), was the most famous shrine in Europe during the Middle Ages. It is the object of Helena's pilgrimage in *All's Well That Ends Well* (see III,iv,4). And James was also, of course, the name of the English King.

How can we reconcile these positive associations for Iago with Shakespeare's evil character? First of all, the name *is* Spanish and thus was negatively toned for Shakespeare's audience. Further, it is a variant of the French Jaques (Helena in *All's Well That Ends Well* refers to herself as "Saint Jaques' pilgrim") and calls up the various jokes about privies connected with this name and explained earlier.[18] Since the foul smells associated with privies were thought to result in the melancholic humour which, in turn, resulted in unaccountable actions, Iago's name might tag the character's disposition and motivation for evil. Finally, Iago may have been intended as ironic for the character, in the way that Bianca is an ironic name. Suggesting purity, Bianca is odd for a courtesan. Iago twice calls attention to her name when he asks: "Look you pale?" (V,i,104-105). The /ia/ phoneme in both Bianca and Iago recalls the same phoneme in Machiavelli, the "evil" Italian who figured so largely in the Renaissance English imagination and stage tradition.

Brabantio's name is not derived from the geographical

DESDEMONA

IAGO

BIANCA

BRABANTIO

region, but rather from the word *brabble* (see *Titus Andronicus,* II,i,62) which refers to 'a frivolous action at law, a paltry or noisy quarrel, a brawl or petty war' (*O.E.D.*).[19] Recalling the last syllable of Caliban, *ban* suggests a curse.

The "ass" sandwiched in Cassio points to this character's ingenuous nature. The name might derive from Shakespeare's familiarity with Richard Knolles *The Generall History of the Turkes* (1602).[20] Knight notes that Cassio "suggests 'cassia', a fragrant shrub or plant, recalling the Duchess of Malfi's thought of being smothered to death with cassia (*The Duchess of Malfi,* IV,ii,223); a happy name for one 'fram'd to make women false' (*Othello,* I,iii,398)."[21] Cassio's first name, Michael, goes with his profession of soldiering, alluding to the heavenly warrior Saint Michael.

MICHAEL CASSIO

A historical note: though Lodovico Sforza (c.1451-1508) was Milanese rather than Venetian, and the episodes of his life seem to have little to do with Shakespeare's play *Othello,* he did have a mistress *Bianca,* his first name was *Lodovico,* and he was popularly referred to as *Il Moro,* the Moor.

Macbeth

With the single exception of Hecat, all of the names in *Macbeth* are properly Scottish. Duncan refers to the 'chieftain's castle' (*dun* and *creann*) or 'brown warrior' (*donn* and *chadh*); Lennox, 'abounding in elm trees' (*leamhnach*); Rosse, 'from the peninsula' (*ros*); Angus, 'unique strength' (*aonghus*); Donalbain, 'white chief' (*dombnall bain*).[22] Malcolm means 'disciple of Saint Columba' (*mael Coluim*), which saint gives his name to the island of Incholm (I,ii,61) and Colmekill (II,iv,33).[23] The above-mentioned names seem noble enough, but not especially helpful for better understanding *Macbeth.*

Banquo's centrality during the banquet scene (III,iv) is the point of his name, not the fact that it means 'white dog.'[24] Duncan

BANQUO

55

anticipates the banquet and makes the name association explicit when he speaks of "worthy Banquo":

> he is full so valiant,
> And in his commendations I am fed;
> It is a banquet to me. (I,iv,54-56)

The 'o' ending of the name serves the playwright as a mournful bass-note for the announcement of King Duncan's murder: "O Banquo, Banquo,/ Our royal master's murther'd!" (II,iii,86-87).

FLEANCE   Son Fleance, too, has a significant name. The boy escapes death, "For Fleance fled" (III,vi,7). Banquo's plea to "Fly, good Fleance, fly, fly, fly!" (III,iii,17), and the third murderer's confirmation that "the son is fled" (III,iii,19), underlines the suggestion of "fleeing" in Fleance.

SEYTON   Seyton is also meaningful in the play's context. A legitimate Scottish clan name, it additionally contains the unmistakeable overtone of *Satan*. Macbeth has lost his soul to the forces of Evil, and it is appropriate for him to have Seyton (Satan) attending towards the end (he is called for at V,iii,18).

MACBETH   Macbeth's own name becomes as bad as Satan's, so we infer from the following exchange with young Siward:

> *Y. Siw.* What is thy name?
> *Macb.*   Thou'lt be afraid to hear it.
> *Y. Siw.* No; though thou call'st thyself a hotter name
> Than any is in hell.
> *Macb.*   My name's Macbeth. (V,vii,5-7)

Macduff contends, "Not in the legions/ Of horrid hell can come a devil more damn'd/ In evils to top Macbeth" (IV,iii,55-57), and later calls him a "hell-hound" (V,viii,3). The Porter, we recall, imagines the gate to Macbeth's castle the gate of hell, and responds to the knocking with: "Who's there, i' th' name of Belzebub?" (II,iii,3-4). "Macbeth" jingles with "death" (see I,ii,64-65; III,v,4-5), and makes a wonderfully discordant off-rhyme with "heath" at the play's start (l.6). The name takes on an ominous sound at IV,i when it is repeated by the apparitions.

Literally, Macbeth means 'son of Beth.' In a play fraught with contemporary allusions complimenting King James I (witch-craft, kingly healing, Scottish lore and history, and maybe others), might it be that Shakespeare is making a point about would-be "sons of Beth"—followers of the late Queen Elizabeth—and usurpation?

But veiled allegory aside, one other point need be made: the play has the most significant *unnamed* characters in all of Shakespeare. The Doctor of Physic, the choric Old Man who speaks with Rosse, and the wonderful Porter all are without names. Indeed, it may even be said that Lady Macbeth doesn't have one either.

King Lear

If we do not count titles, there are a total of only eight named characters in *King Lear* (nine if one includes Monsieur La Far, the Marshal of France, referred to at IV,iii,8). King Lear's own name ties in with the sight imagery of the subplot; like Gloucester, Lear has the faulty vision his name implies. Kent's, "See better, Lear, and let me still remain/ The true blank of thine eye" (I,i,158-159) underscores the point.

LEAR

The name Cordelia, too, reinforces the sight imagery. *Delia* from the Greek *delos* means 'revealed,' and this taken together with the *cor-* first syllable suggests 'revealed heart.' We also hear in Cordelia *coeur de leon*, 'lion-hearted,' remembering that a *French* king has married the father-forsaken girl. An Englishman would be reminded of the noble King Richard, the Lionhearted. The Welsh Cordula was one of Saint Ursula's companions, and most of Shake-speare's sources use a variation of this lady's name. Edmund Spenser was the first to have the form "Cordelia." Although she is "Cordeill" in stanza 28 of Book Two of *The Faerie Queene,* Spenser writes the familiar "Cordelia" in stanzas 29 and 31. A historical Cordell was apparently the good daughter of Sir Brian Annesley, gentleman pensioner of Queen Elizabeth.[25] Annesley's other two daughters

CORDELIA

tried to have their father declared insane shortly before his death in 1603 in order to contest his will. Their plan was frustrated by the loyal Cordell, who wrote to the Queen's Minister. After her father's death, she erected a monument to both her parents. Cordell Annesley married Sir William Harvey—the possible Mr. W. H. of the sonnets—who was step-father to Shakespeare's patron.

GONERIL

By the play's end, even her husband thinks Goneril "worse than any name" (V,iii,157). Indeed, the name Goneril seems negatively toned, and suggests to modern readers the social disease. Regan, too, has negative connotations. It sounds like *raven*, the bird that traditionally symbolized the devil because of its color and reputation for pecking out the eyes and brains of the dead.[26] As a woman's name Regan seems unnatural, coming as it does from both Latin and Irish-Gaelic words for 'king.'

REGAN

EDGAR
EDMUND

In his *Remaines*, William Camden explains both Edgar and Edmund: Edgar is derived from "*Eadig-ar, Happy,* or *blessed honor,* or *power,*" while Edmund is derived from "*Eadmund,* Happy or blessed peace" (p. 50). We are told in the play that Lear himself named Edgar (II,i,92). But what of Camden's positive associations for the name of Shakespeare's villainous Edmund? S. Musgrove notes that "Shakespeare's eye may have been caught by [Camden's] next sentence and this would explain why Edmund does not live up to his name: 'Our Lawyers yet doe acknowledge *Mund* for *Peace* in their word *Mundbrech,* for breach of *Peace.*'"[27] Kenneth Muir thinks Edmund's "name was perhaps suggested to Shakespeare by the Edmund Peckham and the Edmunds mentioned many times by Harsnett [author of *A Declaration of Egregious Popishe Impostures,* a source for King Lear]."[28] Shakespeare's brother was an Edmund, as was Spenser, but these associations for the name would most probably have been affirmative for the playwright. Camden also explains Oswald as "House-ruler or Steward" (p. 65), the latter appropriate for the character, though for Kent no name but a foul one is acceptable to him (see to l. 46 of II,ii).

OSWALD

KENT

Kent has the same ring to it as *Blunt,* and the character Blunt from the Histories reminds us of Lear's follower whose "occupation [it is] to be plain" (II,ii,92). Kent can "deliver a plain message bluntly" (I,iv,33-34), even to the King: "To plainness honor's bound,/ When majesty falls to folly" (I,i,148-149). Like

Cordelia, Kent lacks "that glib and oily art/ To speak and purpose not" (I,i,224-225). He chooses a noble Roman pseudonym, Caius, for an alias while loyally serving his unfortunate king.

During the course of the play, Albany grows into an affirmative character. Ancient Scotland was called Albany and was ruled at one time by Albanacte. Camden defines *Alban* as '*White* or *High*' in *Remaines* (p. 41). He also notes that Saint Albans was the first British martyr (see *Henry VI, Part 2*, I,ii,57).

ALBANY

Along with Kent and Albany, the other titled but unnamed characters are Cornwall, Gloucester, France, and "wat'rish Burgundy" (I,i,258). The Fool doesn't need a name. He functions for the play in terms of his role; his character is metaphor enough.

Antony and Cleopatra

The world of *Antony and Cleopatra* is wide: settings include Alexandria, Rome, Sicily, and the battlefield of Actium. There are numerous characters populating this world. Not all of the names on the Egyptian side are purely Egyptian, but all are exotic to English ears: Cleopatra, Charmian, Iras, Alexas, Mardian, Seleucus, and Diomedes. Greek names intrude here as they do on the Roman side: Eros, Decretas, Menas, Menecrates, Demetrius, Philo, and so on.

Octavius, Octavia, and Sextus are names derived from numbers. Octavius and his half-sister Octavia are both eighth-born children. The name Enobarbus means, literally, 'red beard.'

OCTAVIUS
OCTAVIA
SEXTUS
ENOBARBUS

When Enobarbus deserts Antony and ultimately dies, Shakespeare creates another character to fill his place—the soldier Scarus. His name is not to be found in Plutarch but is especially apt, for it is he who reports the "scars" to Antony's honor during the first sea battle:

SCARUS

> She [Cleopatra] once being loof'd,
> The noble ruin of her magic, Antony,

> Claps on his sea-wing, and (like a doting mallard),
> Leaving the fight in heighth, flies after her.
> I never saw an action of such shame;
> Experience, manhood, honor, ne'er before
> Did violate so itself.   (III,x,17-23)

Scarus continues his noble speech at IV,viii, where he appears wounded. Perhaps the unnamed "soldier" whose scars Antony notices is meant to be this same Scarus (IV,v,2).

MENAS
MENECRATES

The pirates Menas and Menecrates are historical figures with names, so thinks Knight, deriving from the Latin stem *minax* for 'threatening.'[29] The Greek root *men,* however, means 'desire' and seems more apropos. *Men* with *krat* would yield something akin to 'desire for authority, might, or rule.' Euphronius, the schoolmas-

EUPHRONIUS

ter-ambassador from Antony to Caesar, has a name suggesting 'good-natured,' from the Greek *euphron.* His counterpart, Caesar's

THIDIAS

messenger to Cleopatra, is Thidias (Thyreus in some editions); this name is similar to *thaddeus,* the Aramaic word for 'praise.'

MARK ANTONY

We have spoken of Mark Antony's name in reference to *Julius Caesar* previously: "in his name, [is]/ That magical word of war" (III,i,30-31). But Antony has not concerned himself with war,

PHILO

as his well named follower Philo, from the Greek *philos* for 'friend,' observes at the start of the play. Indeed, Antony's capitulation to love is underlined by his other attendant, Eros, suitably named for

EROS

the love god. When Antony despairs following his flight from the sea battle, it is Eros who asks Cleopatra to "comfort him" (III,xi,25). Before the second battle, Eros is called to bring Antony's armor (IV,iv,1-3), perhaps somewhat ironically because of its uselessness against Cupid's arrows. And, finally, Eros is invoked when all seems lost because of love:

> O this false soul of Egypt! this grave charm,
> Whose eye beck'd forth my wars and call'd them home,
> Whose bosom was my crownet, my chief end,
> Like a right gipsy, hath at fast and loose
> Beguil'd me to the very heart of loss.
> What, Eros, Eros!   (IV,xii,25-30)

The god of love has vanquished Antony, and he asks the symbolically named Eros to finish him off with Roman honor. Antony's iteration of the name "Eros" in the dialogue of IV, xiv is striking. Presumably a former slave, Antony has freed his Eros (l. 81), but ironically Antony has been enslaved by the like-named love god. After Eros kills himself rather than his master, Antony responds with a speech deliberately ambiguous:

> Thrice-nobler than myself!
> Thou teachest me, O valiant Eros, what
> I should, and thou couldst not. My queen and Eros
> Have by their brave instruction got upon me
> A nobleness in record; but I will be
> A bridegroom in my death, and run into't
> As to a lover's bed. Come then; and, Eros,
> Thy master dies thy scholar.   (IV,xiv,95-102)

From the stage, the name Iras would sound remarkably close to Eros.[30] Thus, Cleopatra, who like Antony has also given "all for love," has a corresponding attendant at the end. The 'a' in Ir*a*s transposes the Greek Ir*i*s into something more exotic. Iris is the rainbow goddess, referred to in *All's Well That Ends Well* as the "messenger of wet,/ The many-color'd Iris" (I,iii,151-152). Corresponding with Antony's 'friend' Philo is Charmian, Cleopatra's other lady in waiting. Her name is from the Greek *chárma* for 'joy,' but more obviously suggests the "charm" associated with Cleopatra.

Although Cleopatra is Egypt's queen, historically she had Greek heritage not African. Her name combines the Greek *kléos* and *pátra* for 'father's glory or fame.'

IRAS

CHARMIAN

CLEOPATRA

Coriolanus

There is a relatively small cast in *Coriolanus,* and Shakespeare finds his characters mostly in North's *Plutarch,* the "Life of Caius Marcius Coriolanus." The exceptions are Adrian and Nicanor who are in other "Lives," and Cotus whose name is found in the *Commentaries* of Julius Caesar.

CAIUS MARTIUS

As we have discussed elsewhere, the names Caius and Martius are appropriately soldierly. The association of Martius with the war god Mars is underlined in the play by Coriolanus' appeals to his god: "Now, Mars, I prithee make us quick in work" (I,iv,10). When Aufidius taunts after he has spared Rome, Coriolanus expresses his disbelief, "Hear'st thou, Mars?" (V,vi,99), to which Aufidius bitingly replies, "Name not the god, thou boy of tears!" (V,vi,100). Earlier Aufidius had referred to the proud warrior as Mars himself (IV,v,118); indeed, in the same scene, a servant notices that he is treated by the Volscian Senators "as if he were son and heir to Mars" (IV,v,191-192).

CORIOLANUS

The sur-addition "Coriolanus" is awarded to the Roman hero with these words:

> ... from this time,
> For what he did before Corioles, call him,
> With all th' applause and clamor of the host,
> Martius Caius Coriolanus! Bear
> Th' addition nobly ever! (I,ix,62-66)

An interesting touch by Shakespeare is that immediately after the new title has been given, Coriolanus asks for the pardon of his sometime host in Corioli but *forgets his name* (I,ix,82-91)!

The Herald announces the hero to Rome complete with sur-addition:

> Know, Rome, that all alone Martius did fight
> Within Corioles gates; where he hath won,
> With fame, a name to Martius Caius; these
> In honor follows Coriolanus.
> Welcome to Rome, renowned Coriolanus! (II,i,162-166)

A few lines later, his beaming mother, feigning hesitation, under-scores the new name:

> My gentle Martius, worthy Caius, and
> By deed-achieving honor newly nam'd—
> What is it?—Coriolanus must I call thee?—   (II,i,172-174)

This reinforcement of the honorable sur-addition makes its omission by the people's tribunes all the more slighting (see III,i,194,210). Aufidius, too, neglects the title in an obvious way at various places in IV,v (102,106,126,147), after the following significant exchange:

> *Auf.* Whence com'st thou? What wouldst thou? Thy name?
> Why speak'st not? Speak, man: What's thy name?
> *Cor.* [*Unmuffling.*]   If, Tullus,
> Not yet thou know'st me, and, seeing me, dost not
> Think me for the man I am, necessity
> Commands me name myself.
> *Auf.*   What is thy name?
> *Cor.* A name unmusical to the Volscians' ears,
> And harsh in sound to thine.
> *Auf.*   Say, what's thy name?
> Thou hast a grim appearance, and thy face
> Bears a command in't; though thy tackle's torn,
> Thou show'st a noble vessel. What's thy name?
> *Cor.* Prepare thy brow to frown. Know'st thou me yet?
> *Auf.* I know thee not. Thy name?
> *Cor.* My name is Caius Martius, who hath done
> To thee particularly, and to all the Volsces,
> Great hurt and mischief; thereto witness may
> My surname, Coriolanus. The painful service,
> The extreme dangers, and the drops of blood
> Shed for my thankless country are requited
> But with that surname—a good memory
> And witness of the malice and displeasure
> Which thou shouldst bear me. Only that name remains.
>   (IV,v,52-73)

Thus Shakespeare emphasizes the importance of Coriolanus' name. Aufidius is explicit about omission of the sur-addition before Coriolanus is killed:

> . . . Martius, Caius Martius! Dost thou think
> I'll grace thee with that robbery, thy stol'n name
> Coriolanus, in Corioles?   (V,vi,87-89)

AUFIDIUS

Aufidius' own name is played with by Menenius, who tells the women of the Volscian general's luck during an early encounter with Coriolanus: "and he [Aufidius] had stay'd by him [Coriolanus], I would not have been so fidius'd [i.e. thrashed] for all the chests in Corioles, and the gold that's in them" (II,i,130-132).

SICINIUS VELUTUS

The *Sic-* syllable of Sicinius Velutus is unpleasant to English ears, and the implication of 'young brutishness' in the name Junius Brutus is also negatively toned. At one point in the play, Coriolanus' contempt for the Roman masses is expressed by his generalizing them as "Hob and Dick" (II,iii,116). Shakespeare takes liberties here with his Roman setting.

JUNIUS BRUTUS

VOLUMNIA

VIRGILIA

VALERIA

Finally, the three women in the play have alliterative names: Volumnia, Virgilia, and Valeria. Volumnia speaks volumes as compared with her more reticent counterparts. The 'a' endings for the names are of course feminine.

Timon of Athens

Shakespeare takes almost every name in *Timon of Athens* from North's *Plutarch*.[31] The 1579 edition of this source work even italicized the names for the playwright so that they might easily be picked out. Shakespeare found Timon, Apemantus, and Alcibiades in the "Life of Marcus Antonius," and other names scattered in other "Lives": Timandra appears in "Alcibiades," Lucullus and Flaminius are themselves subjects for "Lives," Servilius, Lucilius,

Ventidius, Philotus, Flavius, Hortensius, Caphis, Sempronius, Varro, Isidorus (Isidore in the play), Lucius, and Titus are all mentioned. Indeed, the only name not to be found in *Plutarch* is Phrynia. It is, however, very close in spelling to the place name *Phrygia* (and to the name of the hetaera *Phyrne*) which Shakespeare would have read near the name Timandra which he uses: "Now was Alcibiades in a certain village of Phrýgia, with a concubine of his called Timandra."[32] Phrynia and Timandra are both concubines in the play. One *Phrynicus* is also mentioned in *Plutarch*, and this name as well might have contributed to "Phrynia."[33]

PHRYNIA

Timon is from the Greek *timé* which denotes 'honor, value, worth, or reward.' The Timon of the early part of the play is honored and valued for the wrong reasons by his false friends. The later more celebrated Timon comes from the character given him in classical literature: the prototypical misanthrope. There is a reference to this Timon in *Love's Labor's Lost* (IV,iii,168), and it is this character who blasts his false friends with all sorts of nasty names:

TIMON

> You knot of mouth-friends! . . .
> . . .
> Most smiling, smooth, detested parasites,
> Courteous destroyers, affable wolves, meek bears,
> You fools of fortune, trencher-friends, time's flies,
> Cap-and-knee slaves, vapors, and minute-jacks!
> (III,vi, 89-97)

As the word *cynic* is derived from the Greek word *kynos* for 'dog,' the churlish and cynical philosopher Apemantus is besieged with dog references in the play. A "dog-ape" is a baboon (see *As You Like It*, II,v,27), combining the dog references with the first syllable of Apemantus. The philosopher sees man as bestial and animalistic: "The strain of man's bred out/ Into baboon and monkey" (I,i,250-251). The last part of the cynic's name suggests the "praying" insect, and is Greek for 'soothsayer or foreboder.' It is Apemantus who warns Timon of the future at the beginning of the action.[34]

APEMANTUS

The names of the two women in the play are also Greek. We have already spoken of Phrynia. Timandra's name echoes

TIMANDRA

65

Timon's. Shakespeare's hint may be that Timon's early generosity is to be taken as tainted in the same way as Timandra's current sexual liberality. "Art thou Timandra?" Timon asks (IV,iii,82). "Be a whore still. They love thee not that use thee" (IV,iii,84).[35] The mythological Timandra was the daughter of Tyndareus and Leda, and the sister of Helen and Clytemnestra. She was a notorious adulteress, and thus consistent with the character Timon gives her. However, she is afforded a certain honor and nobility in *Plutarch* because of her pains at the burial of Alcibiades: "Timandra went and took his body which she wrapped up in the best linen she had, and buried him as honourably as she could possible, with such things as she had, and could get together."[36]

The fact that a play set in Athens should have so many Roman names for characters is remarkable, but Shakespeare could be indicating the late Roman-like decadence of Timon's overly materialistic society. The playwright's fondness for names begin-

LUCIUS

LUCULLUS

LUCILIUS

ning with the *Luc-* syllable has been commented upon elsewhere. In *Timon of Athens* he has a Lucius, Lucullus, and a Lucilius. (Indeed, one of the supposed sources for the play, a dialogue about Timon the Misanthrope, was written by Lucian!)

SEMPRONIUS

VENTIDIUS

Lucius, Lucullus, and Sempronius have names which seem inversions of the light and constancy they denote. Ventidius is as fickle as the wind to which his name alludes.[37] He refuses Timon who had earlier rescued him from debtor's prison. One of the strangers of III,ii is Hostilius whose tag is self-explanatory.

HOSTILIUS

FLAVIUS

FLAMINIUS

SERVILIUS

PHILOTUS

HORTENSIUS

TITUS

The steward Flavius is named only once (I,ii,157), but the servant Flaminius may in fact be the same character.[38] Flavius suggests 'golden-yellow hair' from the Latin. Servilius seems meeker than Timon's other servants in keeping with his name. Philotus ('friend') and Hortensius ('of the garden') are apt servant names. Titus has the sort of grand, out-sized name Shakespeare often gave his servants.

4 THE COMEDIES AND ROMANCES

Shakespeare's comic geography ranges far—from Windsor and Warwickshire at home, to the Forest of Arden and Illyria beyond far away. The playwright seems fondest of Italy, two of whose cities figure in titles of his comedies. Not only Verona and Venice, however, but also Padua, Milan, Mantua, Messina, Florence and, to be sure, Rome are used as settings in the plays. Places French are evoked in *Love's Labor's Lost* (Navarre) and *All's Well That Ends Well* (Rossillion, Paris, Marseilles). Vienna is the setting for *Measure for Measure,* Ephesus for *The Comedy of Errors,* Athens for *A Midsummer Night's Dream,* and there are others.

Even Shakespeare's fantastic settings can be localized somewhat due to the names he gives his characters. Clearly Illyria is Italian in flavor (it was actually a part of the ancient Roman kingdom) with Viola, Olivia, and Sebastian in it. And the Forest of Arden is decidedly French with Amiens, Jaques, a wrestler Charles, and a servant Dennis.

Most of the names in the Comedies and Romances are significant as tags, allusions or, at times, a combination of both. Shakespeare plays poetically with some in the dialogue. The Romances have, on the whole, rather less name signification than the other Comedies, with *Pericles* and *Cymbeline* the only titles taken from character names.

The Comedy of Errors

It is normal for a playwright to borrow from others in early work, and that Shakespeare found some of his names in contemporary and classical drama should not surprise. A Solinus appears as a character in John Lyly's *Campaspe,* printed in 1584; Dromio is the boy servant to Old Memphio in Lyly's *Mother Bombie,* written about 1589; Duke Menaphon (mentioned at V, i, 369) is the name of a Persian nobleman in Christopher Marlowe's *Tamburlaine,* and the title character of Robert Greene's romance. Terence's comedies contain several Dromos (a variation of Dromio), and the Roman playwright's *Self-Tormentor,* in the 1598 Bernard translation, has an Antiphila, the feminine form of Antipholus, meaning 'one who returns another's love.'[1]

Not that drama is the only source for Shakespeare's names in *The Comedy of Errors.* Julius *Solinus* Polyhistor was a geographer who published his *Excellent and Pleasant Works* in 1587. Sir Philip Sidney's *Arcadia* has an Antiphilus, a name recommended for a lover in H. Estienne (Stephanus), *Thesaurus Graecae Linguae* (1572). And Shakespeare might have known an account of the origin of the sea's name to give him Egeon.

The wonderful catalogue of "Maud, Bridget, Marian, Cic'ly, Gillian, Ginn" (III, i, 31) prepares us for the English tag Doctor Pinch. This name depicts the character's physical appearance:

> a hungry lean-fac'd villain,
> A mere anatomy . . .
> A needy, hollow-ey'd, sharp-looking wretch,
> A living dead man.   (V, i, 238-242)

Pinch also recalls the punishment employed by harsh schoolmasters and conjurors' agents (see II, ii, 192).

There are other tags as well. The Greek *drómos* for 'run' yields an apt name for the messenger twins. "Why, how now, Dromio, where run'st thou so fast?" (III, ii, 71-72) asks the Syracuse Antipholus at one point. At another, Luciana wonders "How hast thou [Dromio of Syracuse] lost thy breath?" "By running fast," is the reply (IV, ii, 30-31).

SOLINUS

ANTIPHOLUS

EGEON

PINCH

DROMIO

68

When adapting Plautus' *Menaechmi,* his principal source, Shakespeare makes his "Courtezan" nameless but affords Plautus' unnamed wife a name. Adriana stems from the Latin for 'dark one,' and thus contrasts this character with her confidante sister Luciana, 'light.' From the stage, Luce, the name of Adriana's servant, might easily be confused with Luciana. Thus, Luce becomes Nell at III, ii, 109, and, ironically, Dowsabel later on (IV, i, 110). ADRIANA
LUCIANA

LUCE

Aemilia is 'flattering or winning one' from the Latin. Her name alliterates with her husband's, and is especially noticeable when she reveals herself to him towards the end of the play: AEMILIA

> Speak, old Egeon, if thou be'st the man
> That hadst a wife once call'd Aemilia,
> That bore thee at a burthen two fair sons.
> O, if thou be'st the same Egeon, speak,
> And speak unto the same Aemilia!   (V, i, 342-346)

The goldsmith Angelo's tag name is obvious, as an *angel* was a gold coin with Saint Michael stamped on it. The merchant Balthazar is perhaps named to suggest one of the wealthy wise kings of the Nativity story. ANGELO
BALTHAZAR

The Taming of the Shrew

Like Anthony Dull in *Love's Labor's Lost* and Pompey Bum in *Measure for Measure,* Christopher Sly in *The Taming of the Shrew* has a name which couples the fine and the not so fine. In the "Induction" to the play his actions correspond with his name: he acts a fine lord and a not so fine drunk. His Christian name is from Saint Christopher. The family name recalls both a player in Shakespeare's company, William Sly, and one Stephen Sly of Warwickshire, an historical personage referred to in the play ("Induction," ii, 93).[2] John Naps, Peter Turph, Henry Pimpernell, Marian and/or Cicely CHRISTOPHER SLY

Hacket, and even Barthol'mew sound as if they may have belonged to actual people. They are indigenously English in contrast with the mostly Italian names in the play proper. The sophisticated "Christophero" ("Induction," ii, 5) provides a gentle transition from the "Induction" into the play.

MINOLA

VINCENTIO

The fathers Minola and Vincentio have properly sounding Italian names for an action set in Padua. From the Latin stem *vincens* for 'conquering,' Vincentio goes with a figure of authority. Shakespeare later used the name for his Duke in *Measure for Measure*. Son Lucentio's name, from the Latin *lucens* for 'shining,' is

LUCENTIO

CAMBIO

appropriately positive in connotation for this romantic hero type. But Cambio, the name he assumes for his courtship of Bianca, is even more to the point. He has "changed" his name, and we read in Florio's dictionary that *cámbio* is, indeed, "a change, an exchange, a stead, liew or place." Such meaning is made explicit when Lucentio reveals himself and prompts Bianca's following remark: "Cambio is chang'd into Lucentio" (V, i, 123).

BIANCA

Bianca's own name means 'white and pure,' and she is referred to as "fair Bianca" a number of times (see, for example, I, ii, 175). Petruchio's words to Lucentio at the play's end are thus punningly appropriate: "'Twas I won the wager, though you hit the white" (V, ii, 186).

GREMIO

The old suitor Gremio is named for his intended appearance. Florio lists *gremmo* or *grembo* as "a lap or a bosome" (the Latin is *gremium*), and Gremio is presumably a fat *Pantalone*.

HORTENSIO

LICIO

Bianca's other suitor Hortensio (Florio defines *horténse*, "pertaining to a garden, or growing in a garden") has Licio for an alias which goes with his role. Florio lists *litigio* or *litigo* as "a plea, a pleading, a sute or controversie in lawe, debate, variance, contention."

PETRUCHIO

Petruchio comes from the Greek *petros* for 'stone or rock.' This meaning points to the character's strong and willful nature. As with Peto in *Henry IV, Part 1,* there is also an undertone of phallic implication in the name.

KATE

Petruchio agrees to "woo this wild-cat" (I, ii, 196) Kate, and his success changes her from Hecate-like to deli*cate*. In the early stage of courtship, Petruchio informs his friend:

. . . I am he am born to tame you, Kate,

> And bring you from a wild Kate to a Kate
> Conformable as other household Kates. (II, i, 276-278)

To him she is not sophisticated "Katherine" (II, i, 184), but a

> And bonny Kate, and sometimes Kate the curst; plain Kate,
> But Kate, the prettiest Kate in Christendom,
> Kate of Kate-Hall, my super-dainty Kate,
> For dainties are all Kates. . . . (II, i, 185-189)

The play is on *cate* as 'delicacy' as well as *cat*. The nickname Kate must have had a contemporary reputation for tagging a woman of sharp tongue and perhaps easy virtue, if Stephano's drunken song in *The Tempest* is an indication:

> The master, the swabber, the boatswain, and I,
> The gunner and his mate,
> Lov'd Mall, Meg, and Marian, and Margery,
>   But none of us car'd for Kate;
>   For she had a tongue with a tang,
>   Would cry to a sailor, "Go hang!"
> She lov'd not the savor of tar nor of pitch,
> Yet a tailor might scratch her where e'er she did itch.
>   Then to sea, boys, and let her go hang! (II, ii, 46-54)

Petruchio's Kate is thus not a gentle and aristocratic "Katherine" like Shakespeare's others in *Love's Labor's Lost, Henry V,* and *Henry VIII.*

TRANIO

The Latin stem *trans* in his name may imply the change Tranio undergoes in order to impersonate his master, although the direct source for the name is probably Plautus' *Mostellaria.*[3] Tranio's intended personality, however, might be suggested by Florio's definition for *trana*: "an interjection of mockerie, as we say, nay, tush, fye, or I smell a rat." Another possible name from *Mostellaria* is Grumio. It suggests the English word *groom,* apt for a servant. But we also know that Grumio is of smallish stature, "a little pot," a "three-inch fool" (IV, i, 6, 26). The Latin *grumus* is 'little hill, mound

GRUMIO

71

BIONDELLO

of earth.' Florio's *gruma* for "the eie of a needle," or *grumo* for "a lumpe, a huddle or masse of any thing, a cob" might additionally be apropos. Biondello, the servant, has an Italian tag; he is blond.[4]

CURTIS

Toward the end of the play, we return to some of the colorful English sounding names encountered in the "Induction." They are all attached to servant characters. Curtis recalls the word *courteous*. The others are Nathaniel, Joseph, Nicholas, Philip, Walter, Sugarsop, Gregory, Gabr'el, Peter, Adam, and Rafe (IV, i, 89-90, 122, 133, 134, 136).

The Two Gentlemen of Verona

VALENTINE

There are three characters named Valentine in Shakespeare. The one in *Titus Andronicus* shoots arrows but doesn't speak, and the one in *Twelfth Night* carries love messages between Orsino and Olivia. The Valentine of *Two Gentlemen of Verona* is a faithful lover. All of the Valentines, to be sure, are meant to recall Saint Valentine, the patron of lovers.

PROTEUS

The other title "gentleman" is Proteus, and his name alludes to the mythical figure who could change shapes. In *Henry VI, Part 3*, Richard of Gloucester confesses that he can "Change shapes with Proteus for advantages" (III, ii, 192). Proteus' name signals the character's unfaithfulness as both a lover and a friend, so that the following words of the Duke are charged with irony:

> . . . Proteus, we dare trust you . . .
> Because we know (on Valentine's report)
> You are . . . Love's firm votary,
> And cannot soon revolt and change your mind. (III, ii, 56-59)

ANTONIO

Proteus' father, Antonio, has one of the most familiar names in Renaissance English Drama. Shakespeare had used it for Petruchio's deceased father in *The Taming of the Shrew* (see I, ii,

54), and the name occurs for characters throughout the playwright's career. Thurio may have been suggested by Curio in John Lyly's *Euphues,* or perhaps Thyreus in North's *Plutarch.*[5]

Why there should be two Eglamours in this play is one of those unanswerable questions in Shakespearean nomenclature. Julia has a suitor "Sir Eglamour" (referred to at I, ii, 9), and the name is also given to the character who is the agent for Silvia's escape. Eglamour combines the French words *église* for 'church' and *amour* for 'love,' and is the title character's name in the metrical romance *Sir Eglamour of Artois.*[6] While the connotations thus seem affirmative, the name must also have held burlesque significance in that Ben Jonson's *The Sad Shepherd* and Thomas Dekker's *Satiro-Mastix* use "Eglamour" mockingly. We recall that Shakespeare's character runs when threatened (V, iii, 7).

The names Speed and Launce promote the contrasting personalities of these servants. Speed has a quick wit and tongue (see II, i). Launce, on the other hand, is dull. His exchange with Speed stressing the word "staff" (II, v, 26-33) hints that his name is to be taken as slang for 'penis.' Launce's dog Crab, then, furthers the joke by suggesting the social disease. The other servant Panthino is presumably *thin,* for this word echoes in his name; the name might derive from a character Pandion in Lyly's *Sapho and Phao.*[7]

The "rich Mercatio" (I, ii, 12), one of Julia's mentioned suitors, has his name from the Latin and Italian words for 'merchant.' Although the coupling of the names Mercatio and Julia recalls Arthur Brooke's source poem for *Romeo and Juliet,* Julia may have come from another source play.[8] Shakespeare's Julia here and his Juliets in *Romeo and Juliet* and *Measure for Measure* are all nubile young ladies. Sebastian, Julia's alias, alludes to the young Saint martyred with arrows, and is appropriate to a love story. Silvia's attendant Ursula also derives her name from a saint martyred with arrows.

Silvia, as G. Wilson Knight has observed, is "certainly the right name for a heroine destined to be captured by outlaws in a forest."[9] It has the right pastoral heft. The waiting woman's name, Lucetta, is a diminutive of Lucy (recalling both a virgin martyr saint and Luce in *The Comedy of Errors*). It may have been suggested by Lucilla in *Euphues.*[10]

THURIO

EGLAMOUR

SPEED

LAUNCE

CRAB

PANTHINO

MERCATIO

JULIA

SEBASTIAN

URSULA

SILVIA

LUCETTA

Love's Labor's Lost

FERDINAND

BOYET
MARCADE

BEROWNE

ADRIANO
DE ARMADO

NATHANIEL

HOLOFERNES

MOTH

COSTARD

Because the characters of the "little academe" are so obviously based on historical personages, there is little room for wide–ranging name play in *Love's Labor's Lost*. A significant question though is why Shakespeare, when writing of the maréchal de Biron, duc de Longueville, and duc de Mayenne, changes the name of Henry of Navarre to Ferdinand.[11] Another royal Ferdinand appears in *The Tempest,* so the name must have had the proper aristocratic associations for the playwright. Indeed, Ferdinand was a name borne by many Kings of Castille. Might the reason for the change be that Shakespeare was involved with his English King Henry plays, and thus "Henry" seemed inappropriate for his French setting? Boyet and Marcade, too, are names chosen for their French flavor.

Berowne sounds like the English word *brown* meaning, in one sense, 'sober.' It provides the occasion for Rosaline's pun:

Berowne they call him, but a merrier man,
Within the limit of becoming mirth,
I never spent an hour's talk withal. (II, i, 66-68)

The low comedians of the play all have their prototypes in the Italian *Commedia dell'arte*. The *braggart* Don Adriano has a *Commedia* lover's name coupled with the Spanish sounding Armado. The last name is the masculine form of *Armada,* and would bring to mind for a contemporary English audience the recent deflation of the supposedly invincible Spanish fleet. The *parasite* is the English curate Sir Nathaniel, whose name is appropriately biblical. Holofernes, that "hollow furnace" of hot air, is the *pedant,* and his name alludes to Gargantua's tutor in Rabelais, as well as being biblical. It has also been suggested that "Holofernes" represents an inexact anagram of "John Florio," and thus is meant to identify the character as a satiric portrait of the dictionary maker.[12] Similarly, "Moth" is thought to be an anagram for "Thom" as in Thomas Nashe.[13] In any case, Moth is the tiny and quickwitted *zanni* of Shakespeare's comedy. He complements Costard, the stupid servant, whose name refers to a kind of large apple and is appropriate for a thick-headed

74

clown. Anthony Dull, the constable of malaprops, is given a noble name undercut by a tag description of his intelligence.

ANTHONY DULL

The names of the ladies attending the nameless Princess of France are all to be found in other Shakespeare plays: there is a Rosaline in *Romeo and Juliet,* Maria in *Twelfth Night,* and Katherines in *The Taming of the Shrew, Henry V,* and *Henry VIII.* With Jaquenetta, the playwright may have been capitalizing on the popularity of Sir John Harington's *The Metamorphosis of Ajax.* Jaquenetta, a diminutive of Jaques, alludes to privy, and thus slurs the smell of this country wench.

ROSALINE

MARIA

KATHERINE

JAQUENETTA

A Midsummer Night's Dream

Theseus remarks that "the poet's pen/ . . . gives to aery nothing/ A local habitation and a name" (V, i, 15-17); that is, a writer chooses. If plays are, indeed, poetic "dreams," then Bottom's warning to the would-be explicator—"Man is but an ass, if he go about [t'] expound this dream" (IV, i, 206-207)—goes against Theseus' implicit invitation to uncover the *why* of Shakespeare's choices in *A Midsummer Night's Dream.* The "most rare vision" of Shakespeare's play is perhaps ultimately as unfathomable as "Bottom's Dream" which "hath no bottom" (IV, i, 204-205, 215-216), but one can attempt at least to discover the playwright's deliberateness (and, of course, run the risk of being "an ass").

The "local habitation" and names in *A Midsummer Night's Dream* point to the Theseus myth as a correlative for the play. Athens and its environs is the setting, and forms of the names Theseus, Egeus, Hippolyta, and Titania are common to both the drama and the myth. The wood near Athens is like the Cretan Labyrinth; to this forest-maze the Youths and Virgins come. And there is a fabulous monster here. Like the Minotaur, Bottom is (for awhile) part beast. The name Bottom is a tag for the spool around which thread is wound, recalling the technique Theseus used to find

THESEUS

EGEUS

BOTTOM

his way out of the labyrinth. And Bottom with his ass' head is a kind of Centaur in reverse, reminding one of the episode in the myth when Theseus drives out the Centaurs from the wedding feast of Pirithous and Hippodamia. Indeed, this is the very episode first on the list of entertainments for the wedding feast in the play, "The battle with the Centaurs, to be sung/ By an Athenian eunuch to the harp" (V, i, 44-45). As in the myth, Theseus marries the Amazon Hippolyta (also known as Antiopa).

HIPPOLYTA

The sources Shakespeare uses for his comic rendering of the Theseus myth are North's *Plutarch,* Ovid's *Metamorphoses,* and Chaucer's "The Knight's Tale."[14] Plutarch has both a "Life of Theseus" and a "Life of Lysander." The Latin version of the *Metamorphoses,* in addition to an extensive account of Theseus' exploits, gives Shakespeare his name Titania for the Queen of the forest fairies (referring to Diana, Ovid writes *"dumque ibi perluitur solita Titania lympha"*).[15] When Arcite, in Chaucer's *The Knight's Tale,* disguises himself as "Page of the chambre of Emelye the brighte," he assumes the name "Philostrate."[16] Oberon is either from the old French romance *Huon of Bordeaux* or Robert Greene's play *James IV.*[17] Spenser refers to "King Oberon" and "Sir Huon" twice in Book II of *The Faerie Queene* (i, 6; x, 75-76), a work Shakespeare surely knew. The Latin *oberro,* 'I wander about or go astray,' may be the root of the name.

LYSANDER

TITANIA

PHILOSTRATE

OBERON

Lysander calls special attention to Demetrius' name when he asks: "Where is Demetrius? O, how fit a word/ Is that vile name to perish on my sword" (II, ii, 106-107).[18] Demetrius suggests the fertility goddess Demeter, but this does not really explain for the play why it is a "vile name."

DEMETRIUS

Hermia and Helena alliterate neatly. Hermia's name recalls Hermes, the messenger of the gods, the Roman Mercury. This would account for the character's fiery personality (cf. Mercutio in *Romeo and Juliet*). Hermia is brunette (see III, ii, 257, 263) to contrast with the fair Helena, whose name derives from the word for 'light' in Greek (*helene*). Helena is also the name of a popular British saint, as well as another of Shakespeare's man-chasing women (in *All's Well That Ends Well*). Although the Helena of *A Midsummer Night's Dream* has little in common with Helen of Troy, it should be pointed out that this archetypally beautiful woman

HERMIA

HELENA

figures in the Theseus myth. Theseus carries her off when she is a child, but her brothers, Castor and Pollux, get her back. She then marries and bears a child who is named Hermione, close indeed to Hermia.

Puck is not a name, but rather a designation for an evil spirit.[19] By identifying the character Puck with Robin Goodfellow, the popular name of a so-called "housefairy," Shakespeare makes his spirit non-malignant. Among other places, he read "Robin Goodfellow" in Reginald Scot's *The Discoverie of Witchcraft* (1584).[20]

PUCK
ROBIN GOODFELLOW

The names in *A Midsummer Night's Dream* are mostly Greek in keeping with the play's Athenian setting; however, Shakespeare's hard-handed men have English sounding tags, and the minor fairies names from nature.

Bottom's gang are named for their trades. Quince and Snug are carpenters, as *quince* or *quines* were blocks of wood to be joined *snugly*. Nicholas may have been a generic appellation or a favorite Christian name for a weaver.[21] The meaning of Bottom as the core for a skein is referred to by Grumio when he speaks of "a bottom of brown thread" (IV, iii, 137) in *The Taming of the Shrew*. (But the name Bottom is also a pun on *ass*, an association reinforced by the visual image of Bottom's head. The world of *A Midsummer Night's Dream* is topsy-turvy; things are turned around, bottoms are up. As Jan Kott observes, it is an erotic and sexual world.)[22] Flute's job is to repair bellows with holes in them, and the fluted stops of church organs that whistle when defective; his name additionally suggests his small, flute-like voice. Tinkers like Tom Snout weld or solder spouts or *snouts* to pitchers. Robin Starveling is a thin, bird-like tailor. (Falstaff is described as "no starveling" in *Henry IV, Part 1*, II, i, 68-69).

QUINCE
SNUG

NICHOLAS BOTTOM

FLUTE

SNOUT
STARVELING

Bottom introduces himself to each fairy after he has been "hailed" by them all:

Bot. I cry your worships mercy, heartily. I beseech your worship's name.
Cob. Cobweb.
Bot. I shall desire you of more acquaintance, good Master Cobweb. If I cut my finger, I shall make bold with you. Your name, honest gentleman?

COBWEB

PEASEBLOSSOM

Peas. Peaseblossom.

Bot. I pray you commend me to Mistress Squash, your mother, and to Master Peascod, your father. Good Master Peaseblossom, I shall desire you of more acquaintance too. Your name, I beseech you, sir?

MUSTARDSEED

Mus. Mustardseed.

Bot. Good Master Mustardseed, I know your patience well. That same cowardly, giant-like ox-beef hath devour'd many a gentleman of your house. I promise you your kindred hath made my eyes water ere now. I desire you [of] more acquaintance, good Master Mustardseed.   (III, i, 179-196)

MOTH

Moth is the other fairy in the group whose names together suggest their forest habitation and size.

The Merchant of Venice

The Merchant of Venice settings are handled in the same deliberate manner often used by Shakespeare for character names.

VENICE

Venice is presented as harsh and mercantile, and its name suggests the *veneer* of a superficial city, *venal* in its thrust and *venereal* in its disease. The first three characters we meet in the play are the

SALERIO

Merchant of Venice and his friends Solanio and Salerio, whose name

BELMONT

recalls the English word *salary*. Belmont, on the other hand, translates 'beautiful mountain,' and it is here that the moon shines right for romance and poetry.

The play's title character has many namesakes throughout Shakespeare and Renaissance English Drama, but the use of the

ANTONIO

name in this case may be historically allusive. Antonio da Ponte (Antonio of the bridge) completed the Rialto bridge in Venice in 1592, just four or five years before the probable date of composition of Shakespeare's play. Another contemporary Antonio, Antonio Perez, a member of the English court, figures in the Roderigo Lopez plot to kill the Queen, an incident which apparently gave rise to the popularity of plays about Jews.[23] As well as the Queen, Perez seems to have been a target for assassination by Elizabeth's Jewish physician.

The name of "the good Antonio, the honest Antonio" (III, i, 12-13) might also allude to two well-known saints. Saint Anthony the Great is remembered for showing great patience when faced with many trials, and he remained an ascetic all of his long life. He is the patron of swineherds, and a "Saint Anthony" or "Tantony" pig is a name given to the smallest of the litter.[24] We recall from the play Shylock's refusal to dine with Antonio (I, iii, 33-38), and his reference to *Mark* 5:1-13 where Jesus casts devils into a herd of pigs. Relics of this Saint Anthony are in Vienne in France, a place name remarkably like Venice.

More to the point of Shakespeare's play, however, is the legend of Saint Anthony of Padua, patron of the poor. The generous merchant Antonio in the play provides the backing for the needy lover Bassanio. Saint Anthony's life contains, moreover, an important episode concerning a Jew. Frustrated in his attempts to convert the heretic, Saint Anthony declared that a wild ass would sooner honor the Sacrament. A few days later, while the Saint was on his way to minister to a dying man, an ass left his stable and knelt before Anthony. This led to the conversion of many.[25]

BASSANIO

Bassanio is the alchemist who, because of his rich humanity, love, and friendship, can convert the lead casket to a golden future. Bassanio is from the Greek *basanos* for 'touchstone.' Pure gold rubbed on this dark-colored stone leaves a characteristic marking. Nerissa's reference to him as "a soldier" (I, ii, 113) might indicate that Shakespeare had in mind the Turkish military title *bashaw,* which Christopher Marlowe spells *basso* in *Tamburlaine, Part 1* (III, i, 1).[26] Less hypothetical because he is certainly a lover is the probable Latin *basium,* 'a kiss.'

GRATIANO

Florio's definition for *gratiano* is just to the point of the character Gratiano: "a gull, a foole or clownish fellowe in a play or comedie." "Let me play the fool,/ With mirth and laughter" (I, i, 79-80) he says. The name Gratiano, too, is the traditional one for the comic *doctor* in *Commedia dell'arte.*[27] With this in mind perhaps, Shakespeare named his girl friend Nerissa, sounding like a diminu-

NERISSA

tive of *nurse*. Otherwise, or in addition, Nerissa is simply a designation for a brunette. Florio defines *nericcio, negriccio* as "blackish, blacke, sootie, sable, darke, obscure, dun, swart." Lorenzo has a fine sounding name, from the Latin *laureos* for 'laurel-crowned one,' suggesting him a successful lover and a poet.

LORENZO

LAUNCELOT GOBBO

We first meet Launcelot Gobbo trying to decide whether or not to leave the Jew, and imagining himself the center of a morality play. He iterates his name comically:

> The fiend is at mine
> elbow and tempts me, saying to me, "[Gobbo],
> Launcelot [Gobbo], good Launcelot," or "good
> [Gobbo]," or "good Launcelot [Gobbo], use your
> legs, take the start, run away." My conscience
> says, "No; take heed, honest Launcelot, take heed,
> honest [Gobbo]," or as aforesaid, "honest Launcelot
> [Gobbo], do not run, scorn running with thy heels."
>
> (II, ii, 2-9)

Launcelot Gobbo's ancestor is the Launce of *The Two Gentlemen of Verona,* and his cousins are, among others, Christopher Sly and Anthony Dull because of their oxymoronic names. Launcelot, to be sure, alludes to King Arthur's knight, but it is also a tag for "servant," from the Old French *l'ancelot* for 'attendant or adherent.' The name Gobbo suggests the word *gobbets,* 'small pieces of meat' (see *Henry VI, Part 2,* V, ii, 58), which Launcelot might "gobble" since he is "a huge feeder" (II, v, 46) starved by Shylock.[28]

OLD GOBBO

Launcelot presumably received his Christian name from his undoubtedly English mother Margery (referred to at II, ii, 89-91). His father, however, is Italian. Florio lists "crook-backt" for *gobbo,* indicating a way to play the character. Florio writes "Also a kind of faulkon"—wonderfully ironic for Launcelot's "more than sand-blind, high gravel-blind" (II, ii, 36-37) father. The use of "Iobbe" (Job) rather than Gobbo in Quarto 1 and Folios 1 and 3 suggests the comic "suffering" of the old father and his son while in Shylock's service. It is to be noted that the Church of Saint Giobbe in Venice was and is located near the Ghetto section of that city.

Leonardo, Stephano, and Balthazar are other servants

with big names. Leonardo is from 'lion-brave'; Stephano alludes to the Saint of arrows. While Balthazars are also servant characters in *Much Ado About Nothing* and *Romeo and Juliet*, it is significant that Portia chooses her own servant's name for her pseudonym at the trial, a Semitic name that alludes to one of the wise men and means "Oh, protect the king."[29] This meaning goes neatly with Portia's eloquent defense of Christian doctrine, and is perhaps the reason she selects it. Additionally, Belshazzar, the Babylonian name for Daniel, is given as "Balthazar" in some Bibles, and thus provides name play when Shylock cries "A Daniel come to judgment! yea, a Daniel!" (IV, i, 223). Daniel is Hebrew for 'God is my judge.' Portia's legal strategy comes from Cousin Goodair, "Doctor Bellario" (III, iv, 50).

LEONARDO

STEPHANO

BALTHAZAR

BELLARIO

After Antonio's ships are described "with portly sail" (I, i 9), and Bassanio thinks that "By something showing a more swelling port" (I, i, 124) than his means allow might win her, Portia is introduced: "Her name is Portia, nothing undervalu'd/ To Cato's daughter, Brutus' Portia" (I, i, 165-166). With the casket scene in mind, Ruskin connects the name with "portion," finding in the character "fortune's lady." Florio agrees: *"portióne*—a portion, a share, a parcell, a part, a rate, a quantitie, a proportion, a measure or peece, a partage."

PORTIA

More has been written on Shylock's name than any other in Shakespeare, and many sources for it have been suggested.[30] *Genesis* seems the most likely one; at 49:10, *Shiloh* is used to designate "Messiah" or, more to the point of Shakespeare's character, means 'dissoluing, or ... mocked or deceiuing.'[31] Chapters 10 and 11 of *Genesis* contain a geneology that lists "Sa'lah" as Shem's grandson and father of Eber (i.e. Hebrew). Shylock would be, thus, an Anglicised biblical name. Sa'lah's progeny includes Iscah from the Hebrew word for 'spy or looker-out' (though *yishay* means 'wealthy one'). The Italian form of the Hebrew name could be Jessica, as in the play. The same geneology also includes the names Tubal and Chus.

SHYLOCK

Historical personages with names similar to Shylock have been mentioned as possible sources for the name. There was one Richard Shylok of Hoo (a most unlikely direct source), and a Richard Shacklock, recusant writer and defender of Roman Catholicism (which presumably relates to Shylock's defense of Judaism).[32]

More fruitful to pursue are some of the obscure tag meanings of words similar to the name. For example, the Hebrew word for 'cormorant' is *shallach,* and we recall from Ben Jonson's *Volpone* that birds of prey were common symbols for the greedy. Along these lines, the name Jessica might suggest the *jesses* or reins

JESSICA

attached to a captive falcon (see *Othello* III, iii, 261), thus reinforcing the bird imagery. The *O.E.D.* lists *shycock* as 'a cautious and cowardly person, specially one who keeps himself hidden from fear of officials,' and this seems to jibe with Shakespeare's characterization of Shylock. There is also a word *shullock* (dialect *shallock* or *shoolock*) defined as 'to idle about, to slouch. Used as a term of contempt.' Thus it has been offered that Shylock is not really a name at all, but rather a term of contempt.[33] The Hebrew for Saul or the Italian family name Scialocca could also be Anglicized into Shylock.

LEAH

TUBAL

Together with the Hebrew names Leah ('painful or wearied') and Tubal ('borne worldly *or* confusion *or* slaunder'),[34] Shylock's name sounds harsh and foreign among the preponderant Italian names of the play. He is an outsider in name as well as religion.

The Merry Wives of Windsor

Some of the characters in *The Merry Wives of Windsor* have been carried over from the two parts of *Henry IV* and *Henry V,* but their names seem rather less suggestive for the comedy than they did for the histories. Falstaff, for example, contains only the

FALSTAFF

suggestion of impotence in terms of the action of *The Merry Wives of Windsor.* The name no longer implies a *false staff* for a prince and future king. Justice Shallow still maintains the lack of wit tagged in

SHALLOW

his name, and Nym is yet a thief (see IV, v, 30-33); however,

NYM

Bardolph, Pistol, and Mistress Quickly all seem modified in character and less in keeping with their names. The more seamy allusions in Quickly have no reference in this play, and the name merely underlines the character's messenger function: "I must carry . . .

QUICKLY

quickly" (III, v, 46-47).

In keeping with the Windsor setting, many of the "new" characters have decidedly English names. Fenton comes from the Old English *fenntun* for 'marsh farm or estate,' *fen* in modern English. A historical Sir Geoffrey Fenton (c. 1539-1608) was an important Elizabethan statesman and translator.[35] The Frank in Frank Ford is a shortened form of *franklin,* and the last name refers to a river crossing. Falstaff plays with the name Ford after being thrown into the Thames: "I have had ford enough. I was thrown into the ford; I have my belly full of ford" (III, v, 35-37). Falstaff disguises himself comically as the witch of Brain*ford*.

FENTON

FRANK FORD

Ford's alias is appropriately Brook (although it was changed to Broome for the Folio, probably because of William Brooke, Seventh Lord Cobham).[36] After receiving "a morning's draught of sack" from him, Falstaff quibbles with what he has been told is the name of his benefactor: "Such [Brooks] are welcome to me, that o'erflows such liquor" (II, ii, 144-151).

BROOK

George Page's Christian name recalls the English Patron Saint, and his family name provides another occasion for punning, this time by Mistress Quickly to Falstaff: "Mistress Page would desire you to send her your little page, of all loves. Her husband has a marvellous infection to the little page; and truly Master Page is an honest man. . . . You must send her your page" (II, ii, 113-122). Mistress Page herself has the homey English nickname Meg.

GEORGE PAGE

MARGARET

William and Anne were two of the commonest names in England during the Renaissance.[37] To be sure, Shakespeare's own Christian name is William and his younger sister, who had died in childhood, and wife were both Annes. The impulse to see in William Page of the Latin lesson a satiric self-portrait of the playwright himself, with his "small *Latine*," is almost irresistible. "William" is repeated eleven times in about sixty lines at Act IV, scene i. The allusion in the name could be to William the Conqueror, and since Page is a synonym for 'servant' the complete name William Page would be, thus, oxymoronic. The "sweet Nan" (III, iv, 2) who "shall be the queen of all the fairies" (IV, iv, 71) may be an oblique reference to Anne Bullen, mother of Shakespeare's "Fairie Queene."

WILLIAM

ANNE

The servants have English sounding names as well. The "impotent" Falstaff's page is Robin, Elizabethan slang for 'penis.'[38] The character is small in size to contrast with his master's overall

ROBIN

bulk. At one point, Robin is referred to as a baby sparrow hawk, "eyas-musket" (III, iii, 22). He is as bird-like as Robin Starveling, his namesake in *A Midsummer Night's Dream*.

Why there should be two servants, Robert and John, whose names duplicate Robin's and Falstaff's (see III, iii, 1-3) is another of the loose ends of Shakespearean nomenclature. Peter Simple is an oxymoronic name. Simple errs on his dates (see I, i, 204-205) and is an easy butt for Falstaff and the Host of the *Garter Inn* at Act IV, scene i. Jack Rugby's last name, the same as the rough game, is from *rugger* for 'robber.'

Even the names of characters referred to but who do not appear in the play are marvelously English: Yead Miller (I, i, 157), Alice Shortcake (I, i, 204), Mistress Bridget (II, ii, 12). Cricket and Bede are fairies (V, v, 43, 49). Amaimon, Lucifer, and Barbason are mentioned devils (II, ii, 297), perhaps from English lore. Sackerson was apparently an actual bear (I, i, 295).

We come at last to the physician, the parson, and the village idiot. The high-sounding Latin name of the French doctor is explained by Helge Kökeritz: "*Caius* was merely a spelling of *Keys*, and *key* was doubtless a current slang expression for what he [Shakespeare] elsewhere calls bauble (RJ 2.4.97) or *weapon* (2H4 2.1.17). By this suggestive name Shakespeare consequently gave the playgoers a broad hint of the doctor's specialization, which was further emphasized by his colorful French-English jargon; there is more than one reference in Shakespeare to the French disease."[39] Dr. Caius' own description of his well-born patients—"de earl, de knight, de lords, de gentlemen" (II, iii, 92)—who presumably are more prone to the specific affliction than most, reinforces the point.

Sir Hugh's last name is typically Welsh, and Evans might also indicate that he is an *evan*gelical parson. Hugh suggests *huge* (see Lyford, p. 85), and the character is meant to contrast physically with Slender who is as thin as a slice of Banbury cheese (see *Riverside* note to I, i, 128). Abraham is also slender of wit, and his full name is undoubtedly oxymoronic.

PETER SIMPLE

RUGBY

CAIUS

HUGH EVANS

ABRAHAM SLENDER

84

Much Ado About Nothing

The romantic leads in *Much Ado About Nothing* are all interestingly named, and these names seem original with Shakespeare, as they do not appear in any of his known sources. Benedick is from the Latin *benedictus* for 'blessed.' Beatrice associates the name with a disease (I, i, 89), but Margaret plays with it as a medicine or cure for the lovesick Beatrice: "Get you some of this distill'd *carduus benedictus,* and lay it to your heart; it is the only thing for a qualm" (III, iv, 73-75). *"Benedictus!* why *benedictus?* You have some moral in this *benedictus"* (III, iv, 77-78), questions the knowing Beatrice.

BENEDICK

Florio defines *benedicente:* " a well-speaking man," and Shakespeare's Benedick is indeed well-spoken. Yet Saint Benedict's most celebrated rule for his monastic order was Silence, so that perhaps there is also a twist of irony in the name.

Beatrice, too, is ironic: the Latin *beatrix* is 'bringer of joy.' Florio notes that *Beatrice,* a woman's name, means "a she happie-maker" (1611 edition). Benedick might argue with these definitions when related to his lady's character—at least at first where he refers to her as "my dear Lady Disdain" (I, i, 118) and "my Lady Tongue" (II, i, 275). But in the end, Beatrice is true to her name.

BEATRICE

Claudio is a traditional *Commedia dell'arte* lover's name, and Shakespeare uses it for another young man in *Measure for Measure.* Despite this Claudio's description as "the right noble Claudio" (I, i, 84-85), there are unpleasant aspects to the character and these are reflected in his name. Claudio's willingness to believe the accusations against Hero suggest that he is something of a thick-headed *clotpole.* He is less than upright in his dealings with his would-be bride, and the Latin *claudus* for 'lame' might signal a spiritual lameness.

CLAUDIO

Barbara Lewalski has argued that Shakespeare meant Hero's name to be an allusion to Hero of Sestos.[40] She notes that in Chapman's version of the myth Venus denounces Hero for pretended virginity. Don John iterates the name to Claudio maliciously: "Leonato's Hero, your Hero, every man's Hero" (III, ii, 106-107), and Claudio repeats it himself when he confronts the character, asking her to "answer truly to . . . [her] name":

HERO

Hero. Is it not Hero? Who can blot that name
With any just reproach?
Claud.   Marry, that can Hero,
Hero itself can blot out Hero's virtue.   (IV, i, 80-82)

JOHN

The harshly English *John* stands out from the other names in *Much Ado About Nothing.* The character's brother is a Don Pedro, but John is neither Don Juan or Don Giovanni. The reason for Don John's name is clear: he is the anti-romantic villain in this romantic comedy, and his name points to his nature. "He is of a very melancholy disposition" (II, i, 5). His cohorts have tag names.

CONRADE
BORACHIO

Conrade is a comrade, 'bold in advice' (Germanic *kuoni,* 'bold,' *rat,* 'advice'). Borachio is from the Italian word *boraccia* for 'leather flask,' which presumably carried strong drink.

LEONATO

For Leonato, the Governor of Messina, a noble name is appropriate, and like Leontes in *The Winter's Tale,* for example, he has one. Antonio is Shakespeare's favorite name for father or father-like characters. Here Antonio plays father to the disguised Hero at the play's end. Balthasar the playwright seems to have associated with attendant characters, and the one in *Much Ado About Nothing* attends with his music. Margaret and Ursula are the names of virgin saints, and the gentlewomen characters who bear these names reinforce Hero's maidenly innocence. Shakespeare humanizes the ladies with their nicknames, "Ursley" (III, i, 4) and "Meg" (III, iv, 7, 98).

ANTONIO

BALTHASAR

MARGARET
URSULA

Dogberry and his Watch have colorful names in keeping with their characters and functions. They are English tags for persons in an Italian setting. Despite his instructions to his troops, "You shall . . . make no noise in the streets; for, for the watch to babble and to talk, is most tolerable, and not to be endur'd" (III, iii, 34-36), Dogberry himself babbles on like a dog-ape (see *As You Like It,* II, v, 27) or baboon. And like "man's best friend," Dogberry is lovable but limited in intelligence. His language is *doggerel* and his interrogations are *dogged.* A *dogberry* is, literally, the fruit of the dogwood tree.

DOGBERRY

VERGES
HUGH OATCAKE

The headborough Verges gets his name from the *verge* or staff of office which he presumably carries. Hugh Oatcake is an oxymoronic name. Hugh is from the Old English *hugi* meaning 'intelligence,' surely ironic for the character, and this lofty Christian

86

name clashes cacophonously against plain Oatcake. "God hath blest you with a good name" (III, iii, 13-14), says Dogberry of George Seacole. He is correct: the George is from the name of the English Patron Saint, and *sea-coal* is quality fuel (see *The Merry Wives of Windsor*, I, iv, 9).The usual coal was charcoal, not the more expensive variety mined and brought by sea from the north of England. George, from the Greek *georgos,* signifies 'farmer.'

GEORGE SEACOLE

As You Like It

S.A. Tannenbaum has correctly observed "the fact that almost every name occurring in *As You Like It* is a significant name."[41] Many of them are French to go with the Arden setting, the present-day Ardennes of France, Belgium, and Luxembourg. But a few of the names are English, and suggest that Shakespeare also had in mind the forest of Arden in his native Warwickshire.

Jaques is slang for 'privy' (see *King Lear,* II, ii, 66-67), and we have explained before that this association was popularized in Sir John Harington's *The Metamorphosis of Ajax.* Because Renaissance English privies were so noisome smelling, the melancholic humour was associated with them—bad smells were thought to induce melancholy. Travel, too, resulted in melancholy, presumably because home was dull after a good trip. Thus, the melancholy Jaques is referred to as "Monsieur Traveller" (IV, i, 33) by Rosalind.

JAQUES

It is, however, the other Jaques who is travelling throughout most of the play, and when this character finally appears he does not seem at all melancholy. Why Shakespeare has two Jaques in *As You Like It*—and, for that matter, why he has two Olivers—is puzzling. He has taken care to change Thomas Lodge's Rosander (found in the source narrative *Rosalynde, or Euphues' Golden Legacy*) to Orlando, perhaps to avoid confusion with Rosalind on hearing. But if this is true, he is careful in one place and not in others. To avoid mixing up the two Jaques, German editors sometimes change Jaques de Boys' name in their texts. Yet an example of confusion compounded occurs in a nineteenth-century edition of *Shakespeare's Dramatische Werke* where, in this Schlegel translation, "Jakob" is listed among the *Personen* but "Jaques de Boys" in the text of the play itself.[42]

DUKE SENIOR

FREDERICK

Duke Senior's name in Lodge's novel is Gerismond, from the Greek *geras* for 'old age.' The "Senior" designation by Shakespeare recalls this source name vaguely. Brother Duke Frederick is named ironically, as the name is from the Gothic for 'peaceful ruler' (*frithuric*). In *Remaines* Camden defines *Frederic* as "Rich peace" (p. 53). Tannenbaum hypothesizes that perhaps the name Frederick "was intended for the banished Duke and that something went wrong either in the composition of the play or during a revision."[43] But the name might rather be intended to signal the character's religious conversion and reformation at the play's end. Too, the German Frederick Count Mompelgard, who figures as an object for parody in *The Merry Wives of Windsor,* was still subject matter for the English court at the time of *As You Like It.*[44] Hence, the name Frederick could be in addition a contemporary reference.

OLIVER

LE BEAU

Oliver may also function as a name suggesting reformation, connoting this wicked brother's conversion to the *peace* associated with the olive branch. Le Beau's name is concomitant with his flamboyant character and foppish behavior. His name and the names Amiens, Dennis, and Charles are French. On the way from Paris to the Channel, one passes through the towns of Amiens and Saint Denis. Amiens' name indicates that he is Duke Senior's amiable 'friend' and companion. Saint Denis is the patron of France, and Kings of France named Charles occur in more than one Shakespeare history play. Charles originally derives from the Old High German *karal* for 'strong man.'

AMIENS

DENNIS

CHARLES

ORLANDO

DE BOYS

Sir Rowland de Boys and his sons might recall an actual Leicester and Warwickshire family, that of Sir Ernald (Arnold) de Boys.[45] What is more likely, however, is that Shakespeare had the famous *Chanson de Roland* in mind when naming these characters. Roland is the celebrated hero-nephew of Charlemagne; Orlando is Italian for Roland. It is to be noted that Sir John Harington, whose *The Metamorphosis of Ajax* Shakespeare found so congenial as a sourcebook for some of his names, translated Ariosto's epic *Orlando Furioso* in about 1591. De Boys comes from the French and means, appropriately for Shakespeare's play, 'of the forest' (*bois*). Orlando's faithful kinsman in the *Chanson de Roland* is Oliver, and the playwright links the names in the following lines from *Henry VI, Part 1:* "Froissart, a countryman of ours, records/ England all Olivers and Rolands bred" (I, ii, 29-30).

The name Adam Shakespeare retains from his source, though without Lodge's last name Spencer. Adam underlines the great age of the character, and suggests that he comes from a better world or more Edenic time. The name is the Hebrew for 'red,' the color of skin, and it came to mean simply 'man' (Camden's *Remaines:* "Man, earthly, or red," p. 40). Tannenbaum notes that *man* was 'servant' to an Elizabethan, and thus Adam is a most appropriate designation for this character.[46]

    ADAM

Touchstone is similarly a happy name. The professional fool is, indeed, for this play thematically a measuring instrument by which audience or reader can evaluate the attitudes and sentiments expressed by various other characters. In part he functions as a witty authorial norm, important for gauging tone. Touchstones were basanite (basalt), fine-grained dark-colored quartz or jasper, used for testing the quality of gold or silver. Shakespeare refers to such stones in *Pericles* (II, ii, 37), and names Bassanio in *The Merchant of Venice* with them in mind. The character Touchstone tests the "golden world" of the Forest of Arden, sometimes contradicting the "sermons in stones." He takes the measure of Jaques, William, and others while, at the same time, admitting to folly of his own. He has courted the marvelously named Jane Smile: "I remember when I was in love, I broke my sword upon a stone, and bid him take that for coming a-night to Jane Smile; and I remember the kissing of her batler and the cow's dugs that her pretty chopp'd hands had milk'd; and I remember the wooing of a peascod instead of her, from whom I took two cods, and giving her them again, said with weeping tears, 'Wear these for my sake.' We that are true lovers run into strange capers; but as all is mortal in nature, so is all nature in love mortal in folly" (II, iv, 46-56). Less romantic than his courtship of Jane is Touchstone's wooing of the country wench Audrey. In the sixteenth-century, the word *tawdry* was coined from Audrey, a name favored by the poorer classes, to suggest any cheap or garish goods.[47]

    TOUCHSTONE

    JANE SMILE

    AUDREY

Touchstone sings a snatch of "O sweet Oliver,/ O brave

OLIVER MARTEXT Oliver" (III, iii, 99-100) to Sir Oliver Martext, the country priest whose first name recalls the heroic Oliver and whose last tags his qualifications. The family name is also a variation on Marprelate which Elizabethans would have been familiar with from the notorious Puritan pamphlets attacking the Anglican church. The "Sir" designation in front of his name indicates that he is a clergyman.

CORIN The other country characters also have apt names. Corin would be heard from the stage as *corn*, generic for any 'grain.' The name is, to be sure, the masculine form of Corinna which Shakespeare knew from Ovid. It also recalls Lodge's source Corydon, CARLOT traditional for a pastoral shepherd. "Old Carlot" (III, v, 108, upper case mine) might be a proper tag name for a farmer, and not the SILVIUS description of a mean master as it is usually printed. Silvius comes from the Latin for 'forest dweller,' and is the masculine form of Silvia, a character name in *The Two Gentlemen of Verona.* Shakespeare changed the name of Lodge's source character Montanus to PHEBE harmonize with his woodland setting. But he retained Phebe from *Rosalynde.* Phebe is another name for Diana, the chaste goddess of the moon (see *Titus Andronicus*, I, i, 316).

WILLIAM William has the same first name as the playwright, and one critic has argued that Shakespeare may have written the part of the country bumpkin for himself.[48] We know from the Sonnets that the poet was not above playing with his own name. Linking William with the German *Wilhelm* for 'helmet of resolution,' Tannenbaum sees irony in the name.[49] "Sweet William" is the flower, *Dianthus barbatus,* first noted in 1573.[50]

ROSALIND Jaques does not find Rosalind's name congenial; he tells Orlando: "I do not like her name" (III, ii, 265). "There was no thought of pleasing you when she was christen'd" (III, ii, 266-267), Orlando is quick to retort. Rosalind is for most a pleasant name, from the Spanish for 'pretty rose.' Celia calls attention to this meaning with her line, "my sweet Rose, my dear Rose, be merry" (I, ii, 23).

CELIA Celia's own name comes from the Latin for 'heaven' HISPERIA (*caelum*). Hisperia, the occident, is her "gentlewoman" (II, ii, 10). GANYMEDE Both girls assume significant pseudonyms: Rosalind's is Ganymede, ALIENA and Celia's Aliena. "I'll have no worse a name than Jove's own page,/ And therefore look you call me Ganymed" (I, iii,

90

124-125), says Rosalind. Aliena "hath a reference to my state (I, iii, 127), counters Celia. Ganymede was cupbearer to Jupiter and one of mythology's most beautiful males; Aliena is from the Latin for 'the estranged one.'

Twelfth Night

"Who governs here," asks Viola in Illyria. "A noble duke, in nature as in name ... Orsino" (I,ii,24-27), is the reply. This Duke's opening speech in *Twelfth Night* seems rich in the 'o' vowel, as is his name Orsino and that of his current ladylove Olivia:

> If music be the food of love, play on,
> Give me excess of it; that surfeiting,
> The appetite may sicken, and so die.
> That strain again, it had a dying fall;
> O, it came o'er my ear like the sweet sound
> That breathes upon a bank of violets,
> Stealing and giving odor. Enough, no more,
> 'Tis not so sweet now as it was before.
> O spirit of love, how quick and fresh art thou,
> That notwithstanding thy capacity
> Receiveth as the sea, nought enters there,
> Of what validity and pitch soe'er,
> But falls into abatement and low price
> Even in a minute. So full of shapes is fancy
> That it alone is high fantastical.   (I,i,1-15)

ORSINO

Leslie Hotson thinks Shakespeare's Orsino is meant to be a specific portrait of Don Virginio Orsino, Duke of Bracciano, who was visiting England at the time of the play.[51] In any case, Orsino in *Twelfth Night* is a lover in love with love and, at least at first, Olivia.

OLIVIA   When spoken rapidly aloud, Olivia comes close to "I love you." The name suggests an olive tree. Viola first speaks to Olivia with words that point the significance of her name: "I bring no overture of war, no taxation of homage; I hold the olive in my hand; my words are as full of peace as matter" (I,v, 208-211). Viola, indeed, holds "the olive in . . . [her] hand" after this first meeting, as Olivia falls in love with her.

Olivia is a peacemaker. At various times during the action of the play she stops Malvolio's attack on Feste's jesting, she breaks up Sir Toby and Sir Andrew's quarrel with Sebastian, and she soothes Malvolio after he has been gulled.

VIOLA   The name Viola is an anagram of Olivia with a deleted 'i'. It suggests the flower associated with faithfulness and humility, mentioned in the Duke's opening speech, and also the musical instrument. When reviewing her qualifications for employment, Viola says that she can "speak . . . in many sorts of music" (I,ii,58). Sir Andrew, we recall, "plays o' th' viol-de-gamboys" (I,iii,25-26).

CESARIO   Viola's pseudonym is Cesario, from the Latin *caesaries* for 'bushy hair,' an apt designation for a girl disguised as a boy.

SEBASTIAN   Her brother Sebastian is named for the Saint martyred by arrows, whose legend connotes youth and bravery. Sebastian's association with the harsh sea possibly alludes to the Italian explorer Sebastian Cabot who died in 1557, and recalls a Shakespearean namesake in the sea story *The Tempest*. Sebastian's alias Rodorigo

RODORIGO   (see II,i,17) is like the name of the foolish gull in *Othello*. One of the

ANTONIO   sea captains in *Twelfth Night* is nameless, but the other is Antonio, one of Shakespeare's favorite names.

VALENTINE   The gentlemen attending on the Duke, Valentine and

CURIO   Curio, are appropriately named. Valentine fits into a love plot well, and Curio suggests a "curious, nice, scrupulous, careful, diligent, charie" companion, by way of Florio's definition of *curioso*.

Toby, short for Tobias, derives from the Hebrew *Tob-*

TOBY BELCH   *hiyah* for 'the Lord is good,' recalling the author of the Apocryphal *Book of Tobit*. But Shakespeare's character Toby seems anything but to be associated with religion, and perhaps his name alludes to tobacco or the "toby mug" (depicting a man with a three-cornered hat meant to hold ale). His last name describes what he does (at, for example, I,v,120).

92

Sir Andrew's Christian name is ironic in that *andreios* ANDREW
means 'manly' and not 'cowardly' in Greek. Although the character AGUECHEEK
is a perfect "merry Andrew," a designation for a buffoon or clown,
apparently this meaning was not current at the time of Shakespeare's play (see the *O.E.D.*). Aguecheek is literally 'fever-cheek'
(see *King John*, III,iv,85;1 and *Julius Caesar*, II,ii,113), so the character is meant to be thin.

Malvolio is 'ill-will'; it is a name opposite in meaning to MALVOLIO
Benvolio from *Romeo and Juliet*. Malvolio is a tag underlining the
character's personality in the play, and ingenious attempts at specific identifications for the name miss the obvious.[52] Feste, too, is a tag FESTE
name, from the Latin *festus*, 'festive,' and *festinus*, 'fast or quick.' It
denotes a clown, and also the festive atmosphere for the action as a
whole. Florio defines *festa* as "a kind of simnell, cracknell, or
gingerbread," and this seems to go with Feste's taunt at Malvolio
that "ginger shall be hot i' th' mouth" (II,iii,117-118) despite his
Puritanism. The clown's assumed name Sir Topas recalls Toby's TOPAS
name and the mock-knight from Chaucer's tale. It refers to the
gemstone thought to combat lunacy and is thus a tag.[53] "Good Sir
Topas, do not think I am mad" (IV,ii,29), pleads Malvolio.

Possibly because priests of the Fabian clan took part in FABIAN
Lupercalian celebrations in Ancient Rome, by 1599, according to the
O.E.D., Fabian became generic for 'roisterer.' Shakespeare's Fabian
is a willing partner to the fun in *Twelfth Night:* "If I lose a scruple of
this sport, let me be boil'd to death with melancholy" (II,v,2-3).
Finally, Maria is Italian-sounding (though she is Mary and Marian at MARIA
times) in keeping with many of the other names in the play.

Troilus and Cressida

The play *Troilus and Cressida* has little room for tag name
significance, for here Shakespeare is telling a familiar story with a
well-defined and traditionally established cast of characters. Thus,

THERSITES

while the name Thersites, for example, derives from the Greek for 'son of courage,' this fact is not important for Shakespeare's character. What is important, on the other hand, is that the name Thersites traditionally went with a character of deformed body and cynical mind.

PANDARUS

By Elizabethan times the name Pandar had become synonymous with 'procurer,' true lovers were Troiluses, and false women Cressidas. In the play, Pandarus says of the lovers: "If ever you prove false one to another, since I have taken such pain to bring you together, let all pitiful goers-between be call'd to the world's end after my name; call them all Pandars. Let all constant men be Troiluses, all false women Cressids, and all brokers-between Pandars! Say, amen" (III,ii,199-204). These name associations are teased by Shakespeare throughout his play (see, for example, I,i,95;I,ii,281; IV,ii,100;V,ii,177).

TROILUS

CRESSIDA

AJAX

Perhaps the best example of Shakespeare's playfulness in *Troilus and Cressida* is with the name Ajax. As we have mentioned several times earlier, Harington's *The Metamorphosis of Ajax* identified the name with privy, and the bad smells associated with melancholy. Hence, in the play Ajax is the character "melancholy without cause" (I,ii,26), a "stool for a witch" (II,i,42), and a "thing of no bowels" (II,i,49).

TROILUS

The other names are not especially noteworthy. Troilus is from Troy and there is some banter on this account:

> *Cres.* And is it true that I must go from Troy?
> *Tro.* A hateful truth.
> *Cres.*   What, and from Troilus too?
> *Tro.* From Troy and Troilus.   (IV,iv,30-32)

ALEXANDER

In his usual manner, the playwright gives Cressida's servant a grand name—Alexander.

94

All's Well That Ends Well

There are relatively few characters in *All's Well That Ends Well,* but those there are have significant names. From his source, the ninth novel of the third day in Boccaccio's *Decameron,* by way of William Painter's translation in *The Palace of Pleasure,* Shakespeare retained Bertram of Rossillion (Beltramo of Rossiglione) and the mentioned Gerard de Narbon (Gerardo of Narbona). But most of the names the playwright changed, and when he added new characters he named them carefully.

Camden defines *Betran* as "Faire and pure" (*Remaines,* p. 46), but Bertram is also from the Old High German *berahthraben,* a compound of *berhta* and *hraben,* for 'bright raven.' The bird has ambiguous connotations in that it figures positively in the legends of Saint Vincent, Saint Anthony Abbot, and Saint Paul the Hermit, yet is more commonly associated with corruption, decayed intelligence, souls in darkness, and the Devil.[54] Bertram's clown explains in this connection that he serves "The black prince, sir, alias the prince of darkness, alias the devil" (IV,v,42-43). BERTRAM

Shakespeare added to his source his nameless Countess of Rossillion, the old Lord Lafew, Parolles, and the clown Lavatch. These last three names are tags from the French. Lafew translates 'the fire' *(le feu),* and the false Parolles is "first smok'd [out] by the old Lord Lafew" (III,vi,102-103). The character's temperament is also firey, as evidenced for example by his use of oaths in conversation with Parolles: "Cox my passion!" (V,ii,40-41), "Out upon thee, knave!" (V,ii,48). LAFEW

Lafew notes for us that the name Parolles means 'words': PAROLLES

Par. I beseech your honor to hear me one single word.
. . . My name, my good lord, is Parolles.
Laf. You beg more than "word" then.   (V,ii,35-40)

Though Parolles protests, "I love not many words" (III,vi,84), those who know him add, "No more than a fish loves water" (III,vi,85). Parolles understands many languages, and when he is captured he pleads, "If there be here German, or Dane, Low Dutch,/Italian, or French, let him speak to me" (IV,i,71-72). He fears that he "shall lose . . . [his] life for want of language" (IV,i,70) when he doesn't recognize the mumbo jumbo of the "Muskos' regiment." His confession catalogues a colorful list of names garnered from a variety of languages: "Spurio," "Sebastian," "Corambus," "Jaques," "Guiltian," "Cosmo," "Lodowick," "Gratii," "Chitopher," "Vaumond," and "Bentii" (IV,iii,161-165). Parolles also has a reputation as "a notorious liar" (I,i,100; see also III,vi,7-12), and is a "perilous" (a word echoed in his name) guide for Bertram. He serves "one Captain Spurio" (II,i,42-43) whose name is Italian for 'spurious.'

LAVATCH

The only time that the clown's name is mentioned is when Parolles calls him "Lavatch" in the first line of Act V, scene ii. Lavatch is French for 'the cow' *(la vache),* and the name could have been intended by the playwright as a teasing noncename rather than a proper name for the character. Parolles' tone here is witty and he has been using metaphor (see V,ii,11).

HELENA

The women's names in *All's Well That Ends Well* are presumably all Shakespeare's own. Robert Grams Hunter suggests the same ambivalence in Helena's name that we noted in Bertram's:

> Helena is a beautiful and sexually attractive girl who is also a recipient of God's grace and a means by which it is transmitted to others. It is possible that her name has been chosen with both aspects of her nature in mind. She is, on the one hand, Helen, for whose beauty men launched ships and burned towers. On the the other hand, she is Helena, who was the daughter of the most famous of British saints. Her major accomplishments were to give birth to Constantine the Great and to discover the True Cross, by means of which she healed the sick and raised the dead. Though Protestant historians tended to take a jaundiced view of her story, she was by no means forgotten by Shakespeare's contemporaries. One of the London churches and the parish Shakespeare lived in during the 1590s were called after her and her name would presumably have had sacred connotations for the average Londoner.[55]

Helena's aggressiveness in chasing her man reminds us of Shakespeare's other Helena in *A Midsummer Night's Dream.*

96

Diana Capilet's first name recalls the goddess of chastity referred to often in the play. Diana successfully resists Bertram's advances, and is responsible for bringing him together with Helena. Bertram mistakenly thinks her name "Fontibell" (IV,ii,1), 'beautiful fountain,' but she sets him straight.

DIANA CAPILET

The suggestion that the Widow's daughter may have originally been named Violenta seems unduly speculative.[56] The name is too strong for Diana's character. But the name could have tagged a contrasting character discarded by the playwright.

VIOLENTA

Mariana's name will be repeated by Shakespeare for Angelo's jilted fiancée in *Measure for Measure.* The two brother lords Dumaine recall *Love's Labor's Lost,* another play with a French setting. The referred to "Charbon the puritan" (I,iii,52) has his name from *chair bonne* for 'good flesh' in that he refuses to fast; "Poysam the papist" eats fish *(poisson).* The Steward is Rinaldo (III,iv,19), the clown's girlfriend is Isbel (I,iii,18), the Duke's son is Antonio (III,v,76), Lafew's daughter, Maudlin (V,iii,68); and an Escalus is mentioned (III,v,77).

MARIANA

DUMAINE

CHARBON

POYSAM

Measure for Measure

For a play set in Vienna, there are a goodly number of Italian and Latinate names in *Measure for Measure.* Robert Adger Law suggests that "Shakespeare's mind seems to be still dwelling on the men he has been reading of" in North's *Plutarch,* source for a number of plays written around 1604.[57] He cites the following passage:

> Go call at Flavio's house,
> And tell him where I stay. Give the like notice
> To Valentius, Rowland, and to Crassus . . .
> But send me Flavius First . . .
> I thank thee, Varrius. (IV,v,6-10)

Law notes that "Flavius . . . [is] the name of one of the tribunes in *Julius Caesar,* and Crassus, Caesar's friend, is still another hero whose 'Life' is in Plutarch. Varrius, spelled Varius in *Plutarch,* was a drinking companion of Antony, while a clown in this play [*Measure for Measure*] is awarded the name of Caesar's great rival, Pompey."[58] Kenneth Muir feels that Shakespeare must have been reading Erasmus' *Fumus* when composing *Measure for Measure:*

> Erasmus tells us that a dying man's younger son is dedicated to St. Francis, his elder daughter to St. Clare. . . . In the same context Erasmus tells us that the dying man is visited by Bernardine, a Franciscan friar, and by Vincentius, a Dominican. On the next page to the one which contains the reference to St. Clare . . . , Erasmus speaks of *Barnardino, tandundem Vincentio.* Here the misprint (for *Bernardino*) and the case in which Vincentius appears would seem to have given Shakespeare the names of his murderer and his Duke, Barnardine and Vincentio. The idea of making Isabella a votaress of St. Clare, and the name of the nun, Francisca, may be suggested by the previous passage.[59]

Whatever his reading at the time, many of the names in *Measure for Measure* the playwright had used before. The Duke's name, Vincentio, appears in *The Taming of the Shrew.* A goldsmith Angelo is to be found in *The Comedy of Errors.* Claudio is an erring lover in *Much Ado About Nothing.* Mariana is in *All's Well That Ends Well.* *Romeo and Juliet* has characters named Escalus, Angelica, Peter and, to be sure, Juliet.

VINCENTIO The Duke's name is from the Latin *vincentius* for 'conquering one,' suggesting a leader or ruler. Vincentio's pseudonym, LODOWICK Lodowick, Camden defines as "Refuge of the people" (p. 61), in line with the Duke's role in Shakespeare's play.

ANGELO The Italian name Angelo comes from the Greek *aggelos,* 'messenger or ambassador,' meanings Isabella plays on when speaking with the condemned Claudio:

> Lord Angelo, having affairs to heaven,
> Intends you for his swift ambassador,

> Where you shall be an everlasting leiger [i.e. resident ambas-
> sador];
> Therefore your best appointment make with speed,
> To-morrow you set on. (III,i,56-60)

Angelo also recalls the angel coin, providing opportunity for the character to quibble with his own name:

> Let there be some more test made of my mettle
> Before so noble and so great a figure
> Be stamp'd upon it. (I,i,47-49)

The Duke has just offered Angelo the rule of Vienna in his absence. Shakespeare may have appropriated the name from the character Angela in Cinthio's *Epitia*, a possible source for *Measure for Measure*.[60] The name Angelo is also a traditional *Commedia dell'arte* lover's name.

ESCALUS

Escalus derives from the Italian family name *Della Scala*, 'of the scales,' implying judgment and justice. The character of Shakespeare's ancient lord corresponds with this possible tag.

CLAUDIO

Another *Commedia* lover's name is Claudio. In his Christian reading of the play, Roy Battenhouse notes that the Latin 'lame one' for Claudio is "an old and very apt way of designating sinful man."[61] Lucio is a character *loose* of both tongue and morals. His comic dialogue with the disguised Vincentio (III,ii,86-188) concludes with the Duke's pointed observation:

LUCIO

> No might nor greatness in mortality
> Can censure scape; back-wounding calumny
> The whitest virtue strikes. What king so strong
> Can tie the gall up in the slanderous tongue? (III,ii,185-188)

THOMAS
PETER

Nevill Coghill hears Lucifer in Lucio.[62] The friars Thomas and Peter are named for the two apostles.

ELBOW

The low comedians in *Measure for Measure* have especially well-chosen names. Elbow *bends* the meanings of words with his frequent malapropisms. He is an arm of the law with no brain: "I am the poor Duke's constable, and my name is Elbow. I do lean upon justice, sir" (II,i,47-49). He is not quick of speech because "he's out at elbow" [i.e. without much wit] (II,i,61). The foolish gentleman Master Froth is as a head on ale, tasteless and without substance—surface foam. His tag name is played with in the following exchange:

FROTH

> *Escal.* ... Master Froth, I would not have you acquainted with tapsters; they will draw you, Master Froth, and you will hang them. Get you gone, and let me hear no more of you.
> *Froth.* I thank your worship. For mine own part, I never come into any room in a tap-house, but I am drawn in.
> (II,i,204-210)

POMPEY BUM

Pompey Bum is oxymoronic, combining an allusion to a noble figure from history in the first with an indecent tag in the last. Escalus tells the character: "your bum is the greatest thing about you, so that in the beastliest sense you are Pompey the Great" (II,i,217-219), and he warns, "I advise you let me not find you before me again upon any complaint whatsoever. ... If I do, Pompey, I shall beat you to your tent, and prove a shrewd Caesar to you; in plain-dealing, Pompey, I shall have you whipt" (II,i,245-250). Lucio, too, underlines the allusion with his greeting: "How now noble-Pompey? What, at the wheels of Caesar? Art thou led in triumph?" (III,ii,43-44). Mistress Overdone, on the other hand, calls him a more humble "Thomas tapster" at one place (I,ii,112).

ABHORSON

The name Abhorson combines the words *abhor* and *whoreson,* and goes with the character's occupation (or "mystery," as he would have it) of executioner. The prisoners' names tag their offences:

> First, here's young Master Rash. ... Then is there here one Master Caper [frolic], at the suit of Master Three-pile [thick nap] the mercer, for some four suits of peach-color'd satin, which now peaches him [accuses him] a beggar. Then have we here young Dizzy, and young Master Deep-vow, and Master Copper-spur [simulating gold], and Master Starve-lackey the rapier and dagger man, and young Drop-heir that kill'd lusty Pudding, and Master Forthlight [Forthright?] the

tilter, and brave Master Shoe-tie the great traveller, and wild
Half-can [tapster] that stabb'd Pots. . . .   (IV,iii,4-18)

Barnardine's name could be an allusion to Barnabe Barnes, a candidate for "rival poet," who was charged with attempted murder in 1598.[63] Another Barnaby, Barnaby Riche, published *The Adventures of Brusanus, Prince of Hungaria* in 1592, and his work contains episodes involving a disguised ruler as in Shakespeare's play.[64] However, even without an allusion, the first syllable of the name Barnardine tags this character's animal nature. Ragozine, the pirate whose head is substituted for Claudio's, has his name from the Italian word *ragusea,* 'a ship of Ragusa,' which yields the English word *argosy.*[65]

    The aged bawd Mistress Overdone has had nine husbands, and was "Overdone by the last" (II,i,202). The word *done* in her name is slang for 'copulated,' as in this exchange about Claudio's "crime":

> *Mrs. Ov.* Well; what has he done?
> *Pom.* A woman.   (I,ii,87-88)

Mistress Overdone's nine husbands correspond to a cat's supposed nine lives, *cat* being slang for 'prostitute.' Indeed, one of the "girls" is tagged Kate *(cat)* Keepdown. Because she allays sexual desire, Mistress Overdone is referred to as "Madam Mitigation" at one point (I,ii,44).

    Although their names appear in the dialogue and stage directions most often as Julietta and Isabel, tradition dictates we call them Juliet and Isabella. We hear the Italian word for 'beautiful' in Isabella. The name comes from the Hebrew *Elisheba,* 'My God (is) satisfaction.' This meaning is consistent with our first views of Shakespeare's character. Even Lucio is awed by Isabella:

> I hold you as a thing enskied, and sainted,
> By your renouncement an immortal spirit,
> And to be talk'd with in sincerity,
> As with a saint.   (I,iv,34-37)

Margin labels: BARNARDINE, RAGOZINE, OVERDONE, KATE KEEPDOWN, ISABELLA

Camden notes that the name in its Isabel form is "The same with *Elizabeth*" (p. 81). This association opens a wide area of possible allusive readings in a play where the "duke of dark corners" is already thought by some to be a portrait of King James I.[66] Shakespeare's recently deceased Queen was a "virgin" Elizabeth. Might *Measure for Measure,* on one important level at least, be an allegory of contemporary politics? Then too, Saint Elizabeth of Hungary (1207-1231) has a Lodowick (Ludwig) who figures in her history.[67] With Hungary in the background of the play (see the opening lines of I,ii), and one of the acknowledged sources (George Whetstone's *The Historie of Promos and Cassandra*) about a King of Hungary, the allusions could be still wider ranging.

JULIET   Juliet and Mariana, aside from their Shakespearean asso-
MARIANA   ciations, are names without noteworthy significance in the play.
FRANCISCA   Francisca, the non-speaking nun named in the Stage Direction to I,iv, has a name recalling the saint who spoke to birds, good friend to Saint Clare, founder of the order to which Isabella subscribes herself.

Pericles

The appearance of the poet John Gower "as Chorus" in *Pericles* indicates the principal source for this play. In his *Confessio Amantis,* Gower had retold the old story "Apollonius of Tyre," and Shakespeare appropriated many of the main features of the narrative, even to a number of character names. Cerimon, Helicanus, Dionyza, Lychorida, and Philoten are to be found in both writers. Gower also has a Thaise—which is almost "Thais*a*"—but she is the daughter (Marina in *Pericles*) not the mother character as in Shakespeare. What is most interesting in the borrowing, however, is that the playwright does not appropriate the title character's name. In fact, the name Apollonius and not Pericles appears in all of Shakespeare's major sources.[68]

Because Sir Philip Sidney's *Arcadia* apparently influenced the language of *Pericles,* for a long time it was thought that Shakespeare's hero derived his name from Pyrocles.[69] The sound of the names, it was argued, is similar. Now it seems more reasonable to assume that Pericles, like so many other of Shakespeare's names, comes from Plutarch.[70] Plutarch's life of the Athenian Pericles stressed the virtue of patience, a quality emphasized in Shakespeare's character. The name as it stands suggests the Greek for 'all around famous.'

But the playwright also might have had in mind Periclymens, whose story is told in Ovid's *Metamorphoses,* another favorite sourcebook. Periclymens "had the powre to chaunge/ And leave and take what shape he list," and this ability was "by *Neptune* too him given" (XII, 616-617).[71] Pericles' adventures and the importance of the sea in his story could recall the similarly named Periclymens. Moreover, one of Periclymens' antagonists was Heracles and, thus, "Pericles" might be an amalgam of both mythic names.

A more obvious reason for Shakespeare's choice of name is its denotative suggestiveness for the narrative; the vicissitudes experienced by the hero are underlined by his name. In Latin *periculum* means, literally, 'trial, risk, danger.' The English word *peril* is called up with the name Pericles. In sum, then, Shakespeare changed his inherited name to suit his own narrative.

The names Shakespeare appropriated from Gower are used to indicate traits of character. Cerimon, for example, hints at *ceremony* in line with this physician's ritualistic regeneration of the "dead" Thaisa.[72] The Latin *caerimonium* denotes 'sacred or divine.' Helicanus, described by Shakespeare's Gower in the "Epilogue" as "A figure of truth, of faith, of loyalty" (l. 92), bears a Greek proper name. Lychorida suggests the music and harmony associated with and rendered by her charge. The name Dionyza is negatively toned, recalling the wanton excesses of the followers of the god Dionysus. *Dionysia* were the festivals honoring this god. Finally, daughter Philoten's name, although having an affirmative association ('friendship' in Greek), jingles with Cloten, the name of the evil queen's son in *Cymbeline,* Shakespeare's next romance.

The king of Antioch is aptly named Antiochus. He recalls a number of historical personages, the most noteworthy King

PERICLES

CERIMON

HELICANUS

LYCHORIDA

DIONYZA

PHILOTEN

ANTIOCHUS

Antiochus IV (c. 215-163 B.C.) who figures as the antagonist in the books of the Maccabees. The fate of this Antiochus is described in *2 Maccabees, 9*, a chapter which is echoed in *Pericles* (II, iv).[73] As well as the King's unpleasant historical associations, the *anti-* in his name helps Shakespeare characterize him quickly.

In most editions of the play, Antiochus' daughter is name-
less. However, the Third Folio lists her as "Hesperides" (see I, i, 27). If the playwright means this to be her name, he is alluding to mythic daughters of Hesperus and associations of garden and fruit. Thus, he would intend a reminder of a correlative to the Christian story of Original Sin for thematic reinforcement in his play.

HESPERIDES

The King of Pentapolis has a namesake in the poet Simonides of Ceos (c. 556-468 B.C.), mentioned in Plutarch, who wrote a dirge on one of the Antiochuses. Among many other works, this prolific Greek composed a description, highly praised by the ancients, of Danae and her baby son Perseus in a chest on the sea. The connection may be tenuous, but perhaps Shakespeare knew the lyric or the praise and associated the name Simonides with the sea.

SIMONIDES

The lord Escanes, left to govern Tyre in *Pericles,* recalls two Esca*l*uses in other plays. Shakespeare must have associated these names with authority: Escalus in *Measure for Measure* is remembered as a humane old counselor, and in *Romeo and Juliet* the name is given to the Prince of Verona. Cleon, a common name in Greek drama, comes from the root for 'famous,' apt for a governor of Tharsus. A historical Cleon was an Athenian politician who attacked the historical Pericles. Although the name, therefore, would have negative connotations, it is yet considerably softer than the Stran-guilio Shakespeare inherited from Gower. Stranguilio is decidedly too strong for Shakespeare's cowardly husband. The Governor of Mytilene is Lysimachus whose name is to be found often in Plutarch, especially in the "Life of Demetrius." He was an actual ruler of Mytilene.

ESCANES

CLEON

LYSIMACHUS

Philemon derives from the Greek word for 'embrace, kiss, entertain,' and suggests a friendly servant for Cerimon. In mythol-ogy, Philemon is a name associated with piety. On the other side, the evil Thaliard's name contains in it the English word *liar* suggestive of his negative character. (The Greek Thalia, however, was the 'muse of blossoming happiness.') In Gower, Leonine was the name

PHILEMON

THALIARD

LEONINE

given to the Mytilene brothel owner; in his play, Shakespeare appropriates it for his assassin, perhaps to indicate his feline danger.

Jules Massenet's popular opera *Thais* is based on the story of a legendary Alexandrian courtesan of the fourth-century A.D. She was a wealthy and beautiful woman who was converted to a life of Christian penitence and piety. While her "regeneration" suggests parallels with Shakespeare's Thaisa, the earlier part of Thais' story doesn't correspond and makes the association improbable. THAISA

More fruitful to pursue is the story of Thalassa, a Greek goddess who personifies the sea.[74] If the 'i' in "Thaisa" is a mis-transposition of an 'l', we have *Thalsa*—almost Thalassa. Both Thaisa and Thalassa are three syllable names that could easily have been confused from the stage or by a compositor. In Greek, *thalassa* means 'the sea,' and the Thalassa of the myth is the mother of the Telchines, the fish children. Marina, "born at sea" (III, iii, 13), is a sea child.

Marina's name is not to be found in Gower and is, thus, apparently original with Shakespeare. She herself explains its meaning: I was "Call'd Marina/ For I was born at sea" (V, i, 155-156). Marina may have been meant to recall Saint Margaret, sometimes referred to as the "pearl of the sea" because of her name which means 'pearl' in Greek.[75] One of the most popular of all medieval saints, Saint Margaret's legend is associated with Antioch. More-over, she is a virgin saint, and this would parallel the emphasis Shakespeare places on Marina's chastity. Finally, Saint Margaret is the patron of women in childbirth as is the goddess Diana (who appears to Pericles), also known by her Roman name Lucina (see I, i, 8; III, i, 10). MARINA

DIANA

The other names in *Pericles* are invented tag labels. Boult takes his from the word for 'a stout pin of iron,' sexual in line with his work. It also suggests his quickness. Patch-breech and Pilch are two fishermen, followers of an unnamed First Fisherman. Their names might be noncenames (see II, i, 12, 14), as *Patch-breech* refers to a mender of nets and Pilch, from *pilchard*, is a kind of fish. Additionally, warm fur or leather coats are *pilches*.[76] A "Signior Sooth" (I, ii, 44) is a Sir Flattery or Mister Smoothtongue. Verollus, "the French knight that cow'rs i' the hams" (IV, ii, 105), does so because of syphilis—*vérole* in French. His name makes us think of BOULT

PATCH-BREECH

PILCH

VEROLLUS

105

another disreputable Frenchman, Parolles in *All's Well That Ends Well*.

Cymbeline

Dr. Johnson's scathing indictment of *Cymbeline* includes "the confusion of the names" among the play's shortcomings: "To remark the folly of the fiction, the absurdity of the conduct, the confusion of the names and manners of different times, and the impossibility of the events in any system of life, were to waste criticism upon unresisting imbecility, upon faults too evident for detection, and too gross for aggravation."[77] The play's general worth aside, however, Coleridge saw in the mix of names a preparation of "the audience for the chaos of time, place, and costume by throwing the date back into a [legendary] . . . king's /ia/ reign."[78]

Many of the names in *Cymbeline* are Latinate. Some Shakespeare found in Holinshed, and others may have been invented by the playwright after suggestions from various sources. In *Frederyke of Jennen*, for example, characters from different countries are present when a bet similar to the one in *Cymbeline* is made: there is a Spaniard, a Frenchman, and two Italians from different cities.[79] Similarly, Shakespeare's play has a non-speaking Spaniard, Frenchman, and Dutchman, in addition to the two Italians, Philario and Jachimo (see I, iv).

But Holinshed provided most of the significant character names: Cymbeline, Guiderius, Arviragus, Cloten, and perhaps Imogen. G. Wilson Knight waxes impressionistic when he writes that the title character's name "serves to sound the right note of peaceful and purposeful serenity to which the action moves, possessing a softly shining quality which makes the word 'radiant' (at V.v.475) a natural epithet."[80] He obviously has in mind the word *cymbal*. Knight is again highly subjective when explaining the historical Guiderius and Arviragus: "the first name is a weaker word, though

CYMBELINE

GUIDERIUS

106

with suggestion of 'guiding', whereas the other at least sounds far stronger, with a central syllable 'vir', for strength."[81] Arviragus recalls the noble knight Arveragus in Chaucer's "The Franklin's Tale."

When Guiderius encounters the foolish prince, Cloten invokes his own name and expects it to have a devastating effect: "Hear but my name, and tremble" (IV, ii, 87). But Guiderius is unmoved: "I cannot tremble at it. Were it Toad, or Adder, Spider,/ 'Twould move me sooner" (IV, ii, 90-91). The name Cloten suggests *clotpole* for 'blockhead' (see *King Lear,* I, iv, 46), an association Guiderius points up when he says: "I have sent Cloten's clotpole down the stream" (IV, ii, 184).

Imogen appears "Innogen" in Holinshed and may have been so intended by Shakespeare for this play.[82] "Innogen" might suggest the innocence of Shakespeare's character.

Jachimo is a diminutive of Iago, and both names have the /ia/ phoneme to be found in Machiavelli, a name synonymous with Italian evildoing for Renaissance Englishmen. A clue to Jachimo's temperament is in his name which is the Italian rendering of the French Jacques.[83]

The rationale for Posthumus' name is explained by the character's mother:

> Lucina lent not me her aid,
>   But took me in my throes,
> That from me was Posthumus ripp'd,
>   Came crying 'mongst his foes,
>   A thing of pity!   (V, iv, 43-47)

He was a child born as his mother died. Like Caius Martius Coriolanus, Posthumus has a sur-addition:

> Thou, Leonatus, art the lion's whelp;
> The fit and apt construction of thy name,
> Being *Leo-natus,* doth import so much.   (V, v, 443-445)

So says the Soothsayer. There are many *Leo-* names in Shakespeare: Leonato in *Much Ado About Nothing,* Leonardo in *The Merchant of Venice,* Leonine in *Pericles,* and Leontes in *The Winter's Tale.*[84]

This latter character is remarkably similar to Posthumus; each is jealous, wishes his wife dead, recants, and is finally reconciled with her after a "rebirth."

The playwright also has a number of characters with names beginning with the *Phil-* syllable. Philo appears in *Antony and Cleopatra*, Philostrate in *A Midsummer Night's Dream*, Philoten in *Pericles*, and Philotus in *Timon of Athens*. In *Cymbeline*, Philario's name suggests friendship and love. The Soothsayer is Philarmonus (see V, v, 433), 'lover of harmony,' appropriate for this prophet of good things.

PHILARIO
PHILARMONUS

Luc- names, too, abound in Shakespeare, and there are also a number of Caiuses in the plays. Caius Lucius is, therefore, not an especially distinctive name. The Doctor Cornelius might take his name from medicinal properties found in the cornelian stone.[85] Cornelia is a midwife referred to by name in *Titus Andronicus* (IV, ii, 141). Pisanio is presumably from Pisa.

CAIUS LUCIUS

CORNELIUS
PISANIO

Imogen's false name for her husband, "Richard du Champ" (IV, ii, 377), may be a Shakespearean joke.[86] The name translates from the French to 'Richard of the Field,' and thus corresponds with the name of the printer from Stratford who was responsible for both *Venus and Adonis* and *The Rape of Lucrece*. *Richard* Burbage and Nathan *Field*, we also remember, were principal actors in Shakespeare's company. Imogen's alias *Fidele* is an anagram of *Field*. For Fidele, however, Lucius gives a textual explanation: "Thy name well fits thy faith; thy faith thy name" (IV, ii, 381).

RICHARD DU CHAMP

FIDELE

Guiderius' pseudonym is Polydore, a name from the Greek and meaning 'richly endowed.' Cadwal is appropriately Welsh, and recalls Cadwalader, the seventh-century King and Saint. Like Arviragus' alias, Morgan too is Welsh, from *mor*, 'the sea,' apt for one hiding at Milford Haven. Shakespeare might have adapted Bellaria, the Queen of Bohemia in Robert Greene's *Pandosto*, to get his Belarius. The name breathes the same 'good air' as the setting referred to in *The Merchant of Venice*. Most probably, however, the name derives from the Roman designation for Land's End in the extreme southeast of Cornwall—Bellerium.

POLYDORE
CADWAL

MORGAN

BELARIUS

The Winter's Tale

Although the main source for the action of *The Winter's Tale* is Robert Greene's *Pandosto,* the major source for the names is North's *Plutarch.*[87] Cleomenes (Cleomines) is the subject for a "Life" that mentions both an Archidamus and Antigonus. Dion and Camillus (Camillo) are other subjects for "Lives." Polixemus (Polixenes), Aemylia (Emilia), Paulinus (Paulina), Hermione (as a male name), and the city of Leontium (Leontes) are referred to. Autolycus is also mentioned in the "Life of Lucullus," but Shakespeare found this thief in Ovid's *Metamorphoses* as well.

Cleomines and Dion consult the Delphic Oracle and are appropriately Greek in name. With a Roman masculine ending, Antigonus stems from the Greek words for 'born against,' and foreshadows the ill-luck of Shakespeare's character. Polixenes' name suggests 'an entertainer,' from *polýxenos* for 'hospitable and much visited.' Hermione derives from Hermes, the messenger of the gods. Ruskin notes that this name means 'pillar-like' (*herma*), in line with the character's role as a statue in the play. Camillo is an apt lord's name, coming from the Latin for 'attendant' (*camilla*). In Latin *aemilia* is 'flattering or winning one,' whence derives Emilia's name. The Latin *paulus* together with the *-ina* diminutive indicates that Paulina is of the smallest stature. Leontes suggests lionlike—a good name for a ruler. It also might imply a 'churlish disposition,' which would fit Shakespeare's character in the early part of the play.[88]

Autolycus himself explains the reference in his name: "My father nam'd me Autolycus, who being, as I am, litter'd under Mercury, was likewise a snapper-up of unconsider'd trifles" (IV, iii, 24-26). The Autolycus of myth Shakespeare found in Ovid; he was the son of Mercury and Chinone, and inherited one of his father's lesser known attributes. On the first day of his life, Mercury had stolen Apollo's cattle and, thus, became the patron of pickpockets and thieves. Ovid reports the son as follows:

CLEOMINES

DION

ANTIGONUS

POLIXENES

HERMIONE

CAMILLO

EMILIA

PAULINA

LEONTES

AUTOLYCUS

> *Awtolychus* . . . provde a wyly pye,
> And such a fellow as in theft and filching had no peere.
> He was his fathers owne sonne right: he could mennes

> eyes so bleere,
> As for too make ye black things whyght, and whyght
> things black appeere.
> (*Metamorphoses,* XI, 359-363)[89]

MAMILLIUS
FLORIZEL
DORICLES
MOPSA
DORCAS
PERDITA

Mamillius withers when removed from his mother's nourishing presence. Florizel is a masculine diminutive transposition of Flora, the goddess' name. The Greek Doricles, Florizel's assumed name, is pastoral sounding, as are the more traditional Mopsa and Dorcas. A *dorkás* is a 'roe or gazelle.'

Shakespeare invented the name Perdita after a suggestive phrase in Greene's *Pandosto.*[90] The mother Hermione asks,

> for the babe
> Is counted lost for ever, Perdita
> I prithee call't. (III, iii, 32-34)

Thus, Perdita is named in the manner of Marina and Miranda (in Shakespeare's next Romance).

JULIO ROMANO

The "rare Italian master [artist], Julio Romano," mentioned at V, ii, 97, was an actual and famous artist, who died in 1546.

TALE-PORTER

A Mistress Tale-porter, midwife, is mentioned at IV, iv, 269-270, and has another of those labeling Shakespearean tags.

The Tempest

MIRANDA

Aside from the mythical masque figures, Miranda is the only female character named in *The Tempest.* Shakespeare apparently invented her name which Ruskin explains as "the wonderful." Florio's Italian/English dictionary adds "admirable" to "woonderfull" for the full contemporary sense, and both of these meanings are played with in the dialogue. After discovering her name, Ferdinand exclaims: "Admir'd Miranda,/ Indeed the top of admiration! (III, i, 37-38). Earlier, at their first meeting, Ferdinand cries "O you

110

wonder!", to which Miranda modestly responds "No wonder, sir" (I, ii, 427-428). Toward the end of the play "O wonder!" begins her "O brave new world" speech (V, i, 181).

There are other tags in the play as well. Prospero is an obvious one. Ruskin's explanation, "for hope," is filled out with Florio's definition: "prosperous, thriving, in good plight, that giveth or receiveth prosperitie, luckie, fortunate, good, happie." Prospero does indeed prosper during the course of the action.

PROSPERO

The names Prospero and Stephano are used for characters in Ben Jonson's *Every Man in His Humour,* a play in which Shakespeare acted. Stephano is named for his stomach; Florio writes: "*Stéfano,* hath bin used in jest for a mans bellie, panch, craver, mawe, or gut." Trinculo, Stephano's drinking partner, has a name suggesting a tiddly version of the word *drink;* Stephano and Trinculo jingle neatly together. An expanded version of Florio's dictionary (1659) points to two meanings for Trinculo's name. His function as court jester to the King of Naples might cause him to be dressed with "cuts, jags, snips, pinks, garding and idle ornaments about [his] gay garments." This is the definition for *trinci.* Additionally, *trincáre* meant "to trim, to prank, or smug up finely, also to quaff merrily, and drink healths, as we say, to whip the catt, or to hunt the fox." In sum, Trinculo's name implies a drunkard.

STEPHANO

TRINCULO

The description of Ariel as "an airy spirit" in the *Dramatis Personae* leaves no doubt as to the meaning of his name, though many sources have been discovered for it.[91] The tag name Caliban is a bit more obscure. Could Shakespeare have known and intended the Romany word *cauliban* for 'blackness' and/or the Hebrew *kaleb* for 'bold one' or 'dog' to inspire it?[92] Caliban is an imperfect anagram of *cannibal,* in which one can also read *Cain* and *Abel* stretching a bit. Knight notes the lumbering quality in the name, as if something has gone wrong.[93]

ARIEL

CALIBAN

A name of many Kings of Castile, Ferdinand (or "Ferdinando" as he is listed at his first entrance [I, i, 8-9]) must have had noble connotations for the playwright. His King of Navarre has this name in *Love's Labor's Lost.* Ferdinand V of Castile (1452-1516) was responsible for a law concerning "*Canibals; That all which would not bee Christians, should bee bondslaves.*"[94] The acting company patron Ferdinando Stanley, Lord Strange, also had the name. Ferdi-

FERDINAND

nand derives from the Gothic *firthu,* 'peace,' and *nands,* 'bold' —
thus, 'bold for the sake of peace.' This meaning seems suited to the
character Ferdinand's boldness in love, and peace role in Shakespeare's play.

SEBASTIAN

Sebastian, too, seems an apt name if Shakespeare had in
mind the famous Italian explorer of the time, Sebastian Cabot. In
any case, the playwright's Sebastian from *Twelfth Night* we remember as also a sea adventurer. Lyford translates the name, "majestical,
or honourable" (p. 113). The most familiar Sebastian, however, the
young saint martyred with arrows and often painted in the Renaissance, doesn't seem to be invoked here.

ADRIAN

GONZALO

FRANCISCO

Adrian is another sea-related name. From the Latin
hadrianus, it means 'of the Adriatic.' Knight's sensitive ear hears
"counsellor" in Gonzalo, "loaded and drawn out to match the old
man's slow and ponderous speech," and notes the similarity of the
name Gonzago in *Hamlet.*[95] Francisco and its variants is an all
purpose name for Shakespeare. There is a Friar Francis in *Much Ado
About Nothing,* a nun Francisca in *Measure for Measure,* the soldier
Francisco in *Hamlet,* the drawer Francis in *Henry IV, Part 1,* and the
lord here in *The Tempest.* That the name was popular in Shakespeare's time is attested to by Francis Drake and Francis Bacon,
among others. Shakespeare uses the name Antonio in many of his
comedies.

ANTONIO

ALONSO

SYCORAX

Related to the Old High German *Alphonso,* Alonso suggests 'noble and ready,' appropriate to the King of Naples.[96] Not so
noble in reference is Sycorax, Caliban's mother, whose name has
elicited much discussion over the years. Ruskin's "swine-raven"
seems to the point, from the Greek *sys* for 'swine' and *korax* for
'raven.'

5 SHAKESPEARE'S NAME

His name is protean. He begets doubles at every corner. His penmanship is unconsciously faked by lawyers who happen to write a similar hand. On the wet morning of November 27, 1582, he is Shaxpere and she is a Wately of Temple Grafton. A couple of days later he is Shagspere and she is a Hathway of Stratford-on-Avon.

from *Bend Sinister* by Vladimir Nabokov

He has hidden his own name, a fair name, William, in the plays, a super here, a clown there, as a painter of old Italy set his face in a dark corner of his canvas. He has revealed it in the sonnets where there is Will in overplus. Like John O'Gaunt his name is dear to him, as dear as the coat of arms he toadied for, on a bend sable a spear or steeled argent, honorificabilitudinitatibus, dearer than his glory of greatest shakescene in the country. What's in a name? That is what we ask ourselves in childhood when we write the name that we are told is ours.

from *Ulysses* by James Joyce

In the case of his own name, Shakespeare would have a ready answer to Juliet's question: "What's in a name?" After all, his writer contemporaries found much in it. Edmund Spenser is credited by some with the earliest reference when he writes, in *Colin Clouts come home againe,* of a gentle "shepheard . . . Whose *Muse* full of high thoughts inuention,/ Doth like himselfe Heroically sound."[1] Spenser is presumed to be calling attention to the denotation of the name *Shakespeare.* The King James version of *Job* 41:29 has "the shaking of a spear" as an image of might, and Richard Verstegan's *A Restitution of Decayed Intelligence* (STC 21361) notes that *"Breakspear, Shakspear,* and the lyke have bin surnames imposed upon the first bearers of them for *valour and feats of arms"* (p. 294).

The most familiar allusion is Robert Greene's unfriendly one about the "upstart crow . . . Shake-scene." It appeared in his posthumously published pamphlet: *Greene's Groatsworth of Wit, Bought with a Million of Repentance* (STC 12245). Speaking in 1592 to Christopher Marlowe, and perhaps Thomas Nashe and George Peele, Greene warns of actors, "Puppets . . . that spake from our mouths. . . . Yes, trust them not," he continues, "for there is an upstart Crow, beautified with our feathers, that with his *Tygers hart wrapt in a Players hyde,* supposes he is as well able to bombast out a blanke verse as the best of you: and being an absolute Johannes fac totum, is in his owne conceit the onely Shake-scene in a country."[2] To make his allusion unquestionably clear, Greene has parodied Shakespeare's line from *Henry VI, Part 3:* "O tiger's heart wrapp'd in a woman's hide!" (I, iv, 137).

On the friendlier side is Ben Jonson's First Folio poem. Jonson writes of Shakespeare's "well torned, and true filed lines," then punningly adds, "In each of which, he seemes to shake a Lance,/ As brandish't at the eyes of Ignorance." In this connection, we recall the playwright's comic Launce of *The Two Gentlemen of Verona* and Launcelot from *The Merchant of Venice.*

Shakespeare played with his own name. He does so in Sonnet 135:

> Whoever hath her wish, thou hast thy *Will,*
> And *Will* to boot, and *Will* in overplus;
> More than enough am I that vex thee still,
> To thy sweet will making addition thus.
> Wilt thou, whose will is large and spacious,
> Not once vouchsafe to hide my will in thine?
> Shall will in others seem right gracious,
> And in my will no fair acceptance shine?
> The sea, all water, yet receives rain still,
> And in abundance addeth to his store,
> So thou being rich in *Will* add to thy *Will*

> One will of mine to make thy large *Will* more.
> Let no unkind, no fair beseechers kill;
> Think all but one, and me in that one *Will*.

Here the poet plays his Christian name against the familiar contemporary proverb: "A woman will have her will." Shakespeare does the same thing in his next sonnet, 136:

> If thy soul check thee that I come so near,
> Swear to thy blind soul that I was thy *Will*,
> And will, thy soul knows, is admitted there;
> Thus far for love my love-suit, sweet, fulfill.
> *Will* will fulfill the treasure of thy love,
> Ay, fill it full with wills, and my will one.
> . . .
> Make but my name thy love, and love that still,
> And then thou lovest me, for my name is *Will*.

The first line of the couplet in Sonnet 143, "So will I pray that thou mayst have thy *Will*," puns in exactly the same manner.

Not only in the sonnets, but also with characters named William in the plays can we detect self-parody by Shakespeare. Touchstone asks the country bumpkin in *As You Like It*, "Is thy name William?" "William, sir," is the reply. "A fair name," offers the fool (V, i, 20-22). This William is surely, as the "Will" of the sonnets is apparently, no William the Conqueror. He loses the country wench Audrey to his rival Touchstone. Neither is the William in *The Merry Wives of Windsor* a "conqueror" of Latin (see IV, i). We recall Ben Jonson's note about Shakespeare's "small *Latine*." On the other hand, Justice Shallow's "cousin William is become a good scholar. He is at Oxford . . . [and] 'A must then to the Inns a'Court shortly" (*Henry IV, Part 2*, III, ii, 9-13).

If *Arden of Feversham* is Shakespeare's, we have another striking instance of the poet quibbling with his own name. In *Arden* we find a "Black Will" and his companion "Shakebag," "two rougher ruffians never lived in Kent." *Shakebag* was cant for 'thief or scoundrel' (see *O.E.D.*, and *King John* III, iii, 7). Arden was, of course, Shakespeare's mother's family name. But even if Shake-

115

speare had no hand at all in the writing of *Arden of Feversham,* some other playwright (probably between 1585 and 1592) saw fit to attack him in the manner of Greene, who wrote his attack at about the same time.

In the sixteenth and seventeenth centuries, English spelling had not settled into what are now considered conventional patterns, and more than one hundred variant spellings of the name *Shakespeare* have been collected. Spelling a name was a highly individual matter; indeed, a person might abbreviate or spell out his own name differently at different times. No two of the six undisputedly authentic signatures of the poet (some of them abbreviated by space limitations) which have come down to us exactly correspond with one another. The Bellot-Mountjoy suit disposition is signed "Willm Shakp," the Blackfriars house conveyance "William Shakspēr," the mortgage deed of this house "Wm Shakspē," page one of the Will "William Shakspere," page two "Willm Shakspere," and page three "William Shakspeare." Even on three successive pages of the same document Shakespeare spelled his name differently.

Made up as it is of two intelligible one syllable English words, the name *Shakespeare* was subject to another kind of variation, again due to whimsical spelling. By slightly altering one or both words contained in the name, a new name results. Thus, the playwright's grandfather Richard is referred to as "Shakstaff" and not "Shakespeare" in a Snitterfield manor record.[3] One William *Shakeshafte* figures prominently in theories about the so-called "lost years," from 1585-1592, when Shakespeare disappears from view in Stratford and then reappears in London apparently with enough reputation to be attacked by Robert Greene. This Shakeshafte is thought by some to be the playwright, as he is mentioned in the will of Alexander Houghton of Lea in Lancashire as probably a player. Accepting this hypothesis, Sir Edmund Chambers traces the likely route a provincial actor might have taken to find his way into the company of the Lord Chamberlain's Men. C. Broadbent lends support to this possibility by analyzing Shakespeare's sea and mountain imagery in the early plays, and remarking its correspondence with the Lancashire landscape. Recently, however, Douglas Hamer disputes the Shakespeare-Shakeshafte theory with some

116

force, noting that the William Shakeshafte mentioned in the will was probably a musician rather than an actor and, further, that he was much older at the time than Shakespeare's presumed seventeen years.[4] But persons aside, the point is that names were not sacrosanct and inviolable, and common folk as well as poets played readily with them.

Shakespeare created a number of important characters for his plays with names like his own—made up of two monosyllabic English words. *Hot-spur* and *Touch-stone* are perhaps the clearest examples, with *Touchstone* a sensible word taken in its entirety. *Gads-hill* is corrupted from *God's hill. Shy* and *lock* are both meaningful, but do not combine into another meaningful word when placed together. A name to be added to this list is, of course, Falstaff.

The fat knight's original name was similarly composed of two words, *old* and *castle,* and Shakespeare's play on the name Oldcastle, "my old lad of the castle," was never expunged from *Henry IV, Part 1* (I, ii, 41). Not only did Shakespeare change the name Oldcastle to Falstaff, but he publicly apologized for the knight's earlier name. The Epilogue in *Henry IV, Part 2* tells the audience: "If you be not too much cloy'd with fat meat, our humble author will continue the story with Sir John in it, and make you merry with fair Katherine of France, where (for any thing I know) Falstaff shall die of a sweat, unless already 'a be kill'd with your hard opinions; for Oldcastle died [a] martyr, and this is not the man." Descendents of the historical Oldcastle presumably had objected to naming the fat knight after their ancestor.[5] So Shakespeare went back to *Henry VI, Part 1* and resurrected an earlier name; Sir John Falstaff's original character was fine, cowardly as it was.

But, in addition, might it have been that when faced with changing the name Oldcastle, the playwright was aware that the new name he was using was a play on his own? *Shake-speare, Falstaff*—a shaking spear transmogrified into a falling staff? Grandfather Richard was a *staff* and not a *spear,* and a playful *Bill* (or *Will*) who would become at one time a dull *Launce* could surely at another make himself into a *False-staff.* If "nobleness . . . could have turn'd/ A distaff to a lance" (*Cymbeline* V, iii, 33-34), inventiveness could turn it back again.

The changing of Oldcastle to Falstaff called special attention to the new name and made it ripe for borrowings. In 1598 Robert Deveraux, the Earl of Essex, wrote the following note to Robert Cecil, the Earl of Salisbury: "I pray you commend me . . . to Alex. Ratcliff and tell him for newes his sister is maryed to S^r Jo. Falstaff."[6] The sister referred to is Margaret Ratcliffe, maid of honor to the Queen, who was courted by Henry Brooke, Lord Cobham, a descendent of Sir John Oldcastle. Apparently his admiration was to no avail, and Essex's note is meant as a joke.[7] The very next year (July of 1599) "Sir John Falstaff" was again used as an allusion to Cobham or someone else connected to the court. Southampton's wife wrote him in Ireland concerning some recent gossip: "Al the nues I can send you that I thinke wil make you mery is that I reade in a letter from London that Sir John Falstaf is by his Mrs Dame Pintpot made father of a go[o]dly milers thum, a boye thats all heade and veri litel body, but this is a secrit."[8]

The Merry Wives of Windsor is thought to have reference to contemporary personages and events, and some have read Justice Shallow as Sir Thomas Lucy of Charlecote Manor near Stratford. When the Justice, after much play on luces (fish which emblazon the Lucy coat of arms), exclaims to Falstaff, "Knight, you have beaten my men, kill'd my deer, and broke open my lodge" (I, i, 111-112), those apocryphal stories of the poet's poaching come to mind. The Falstaff of *The Merry Wives of Windsor,* like the Will of the sonnets, or the William of *As You Like It,* is a less than successful lover. Indeed, was Shakespeare parodying Cobham again here together with himself? He did change Ford's alias *Brook,* Cobham's family name, to *Broome* in the play apparently again because of some outside pressure.[9]

This raises a less hypothetical point. Among so many other things, the character Falstaff is a satirical portrait of a poet and playwright. He entertains and instructs. He has imagination and wit. He is a producer and director of dramatic presentations, and also an actor in them. Falstaff's function for Hal in the *Henry IV* plays is, we can conjecture, rather a bit like Shakespeare's must have been for Southampton or whoever is the poet's friend in the sonnets. The poet is the "King" of the Bohemian "underworld"—the entertainer, the instructor, the mentor. But he must be cast out when the responsibilities of every day intrude upon the youthful holiday world. Now the poet is seen as the "false staff," faulty prop, weak support for a future ruler. John Davies' tribute "To our English Terence, Mr. Will. Shake-speare" (about 1611) prods us again to see Falstaff in Shakespeare:

> Some say (good *Will*) which I, in sport, do sing,
> Had'st thou not play'd some Kingly parts in sport,
> Thou hadst ben a companion for a *King*;
> And, beene a King among the meaner sort.[10]

A further link connecting Falstaff with Shakespeare is that very probably the playwright was fat—at least when he was older. This we can deduce from the only portraits with any claim to be authentic likenesses, the Martin Droeshout engraving and the Gheerart Janssen monument half-figure.[11]

Droeshout's engraving was used for the First Folio by Shakespeare's fellow actors. This fact alone would argue the likeness was reasonable. We do, however, have additionally Ben Jonson's Folio poem vouching for the portrait:

> O, could he but have drawn his wit
> As well in brass, as he hath hit
> His face.

Discounting the ruff and clothing, not only out of proportion with each other but also out of proportion with the head, what we see in the engraving is a youngish man with rather large jowels. There is no mistaking the well-rounded cheeks.

It is still easier to see the fat Shakespeare in Janssen's monument figure. From Leonard Digges' First Folio poem, we know that the bust was completed no later than seven years after Shakespeare's death. The rendering is obviously of the same man Droeshout pictures but at a somewhat later age. Although the carving is conventionalized and, one might say, "primitive," it unquestionably depicts a middle-aged writer who is without doubt plump. Janssen's stone mason workshop was located in Southwark, near the Globe

Theater, and Shakespeare's family presumably commissioned the monument figure. They must have been satisfied with it, for they had it placed over the poet's grave.

As a final seventeenth-century testament to the association of Falstaff with Shakespeare, there appeared about 1662 an engraving which was later adapted to serve as a frontispiece to Francis Kirkman's anthology *The Wits, or Sport upon Sport* (W 3218), a collection of scenes abridged from plays performed surreptitiously during Cromwell's time. This engraving pictured favorite characters from the plays and, together with the Hostess, Falstaff is up front with his name printed beside him so that there can be no mistaking him. This Falstaff looks *exactly* like the monument bust of William Shakespeare in Holy Trinity Church, Stratford-upon-Avon.[12]

So then, "What's in a name," Juliet? Plenty. "Wherefore art thou Romeo," indeed!

Martin Droeshout's First Folio Engraving
[*Courtesy The Folger Shakespeare Library*]

Frontispiece to Kirkman's *The Wits*
[*Courtesy The Folger Shakespeare Library*]

JOHN LOWIN.

1640. Ætat. 64.

From an Original Picture in the Ashmole Museum, Oxford.

London Pub June 7, 1792 by E Harding Fleet Street.

Actor John Lowin. See note 12.
[*Courtesy The Folger Shakespeare Library*]

Gheerart Janssen's Monument Half-Figure
[*Photograph by Thomas Holte*]

Figure of Falstaff. Detail from Kirkman's
Frontispiece to *The Wits*
[*Courtesy The Folger Shakespeare Library*]

NOTES

Notes to Chapter 1

1. (II,ii,34,38,42). All references to the plays are quoted from *The Riverside Shakespeare,* edited by G. Blakemore Evans (Boston: Houghton Mifflin, 1974), and will appear parenthetically in the text.

2. *The Works of Francis Bacon,* edited by James Spedding, Robert Leslie Ellis, Douglas Denon Heath (Boston: Brown and Taggard, 1860), XII, p. 429. ["Metis, Jupiter's wife, plainly means counsel; Typhon, swelling; Pan, the universe; Nemesis, revenge; and the like."]

3. Ruskin's observations on Shakespeare's names were first published in *Fraser's Magazine* (December 1862), pp. 742-756, and (April 1863), pp. 441-462.

4. X (August 1864), p. 168.

5. Quotations from The Modern Library *Ulysses* (New York: Random House, 1946), pp. 189, 206-207.

6. (New York: McGraw-Hill, 1974), pp. 110-116.

7. (London: Methuen, 1958), pp. 161-201.

8. "Shakespeare's Nomenclature," in *Essays on Shakespeare,* edited by Gerald W. Chaptman (Princeton, N.J.: Princeton University Press, 1965), pp. 59-90.

9. The first edition appeared in 1598 with the complete title *A Worlde of Wordes Or Most copious and exact Dictionary in Italian and English,* and was expanded in 1611 with the new title *Queen Anna's New World of Words, or Dictionarie of the Italian and English Tongues* (STC 11099). Giovanni Torriano further expanded it (Wing F1368), calling it *A Dictionary, Italian and English.* In 1688 another edition appeared (Wing F1369).

10. See his biography, Frances A. Yates, *John Florio: The Life of an Italian in Shakespeare's England* (Cambridge: Cambridge University Press, 1934).

11. (Oxford: Oxford University Press, 1973).

12. The modern edition of the work is edited by Elizabeth Story Donno (New York: Columbia University Press, 1962).

Notes to Chapter 2

1. See Eric Partridge, *Shakespeare's Bawdy* (New York: Dutton, 1960), pp. 174,175.

2. The New Arden *The Second Part of King Henry VI,* edited by A.S. Cairncross (London: Methuen, 1957), p. 109n.

3. Listed among the "Principall Actors" for Shakespeare's plays in the First Folio.

4. Cf. Bullcalf in *Henry IV, Part 2.*

5. See Mark Eccles, *Shakespeare in Warwickshire* (Madison, Wisconsin: University of Wisconsin Press, 1963), pp. 39,107.

6. *The Annotated Mother Goose,* edited by William S. and Ceil Baring-Gould (Cleveland, Ohio: Meridian, 1967), pp. 62-63.

7. W.H. Thomson, *Shakespeare's Characters: A Historical Dictionary* (New York: British Book Centre, 1951), pp. 178-179.

8. E.G. Withycombe, *The Oxford Dictionary of English Christian Names* (Oxford: Oxford University Press, 1973), p. 197.

9. *Narrative and Dramatic Sources of Shakespeare* (London: Routledge and Kegan Paul, 1960), III, p. 159.

10. Ibid. p. 279.

11. But see, for example, The New Arden *The Second Part of King Henry IV,* edited by A.R. Humphreys (London: Methuen, 1967), pp. xv-xx.

12. See Helge Kökeritz, "Punning Names in Shakespeare," *Modern Language Notes,* LXV (April 1950), p. 242.

13. See Alice Lyle Scoufos, "Harvey: A Name-Change in *Henry IV,"* *English Literary History,* XXXVI (June 1969), pp. 297-318.

14. See *The New Catholic Encyclopedia* (New York: McGraw-Hill), XIV, p. 490.

15. See Paul A. Jorgensen, "'My Name is Pistol Call'd,'" *Shakespeare Quarterly,* I (April 1950), pp. 73-75.

16. *Shakespearean Criticism,* edited by T.M. Raysor (London: Dent, 1960), I, p. 142.

17. See Bullough, IV, pp. 436-437.

18. See The New Arden *Henry VIII,* edited by R.A. Foakes (London: Methuen, 1968), pp. lviii-lix.

Notes to Chapter 3

1. Robert Adger Law, "The Roman Background of *Titus Andronicus,"* *Studies in Philology,* XL (1943), p. 147.

2. The New Arden *Titus Andronicus,* edited by J.C. Maxwell (London: Methuen, 1968), p. xxx.

3. Helge Kökeritz, *Shakespeare's Names: A Pronouncing Dictionary* (New Haven, Conn.: Yale University Press, 1966), p. 42.

4. Noted by Law, p. 146.

5. See Eugene Wait, "The Metamorphosis of Violence in *Titus Andronicus," Shakespeare Survey 10,* edited by Allardyce Nicoll (Cambridge: Cambridge University Press, 1957), p. 44.

6. "Shakespeare's Nomenclature," in *Essays on Shakespeare,* edited by Gerald W. Chaptman (Princeton, N.J.: Princeton University Press, 1965), p. 61.

7. E.G. Withycombe, *The Oxford Dictionary of English Christian Names* (Oxford: Oxford University Press, 1973), p. 211.

8. G. Wilson Knight, "What's in a Name?", in *The Sovereign Flower* (London: Methuen, 1958), p. 178.

9. See The New Arden *Julius Caesar,* edited by T.S. Dorsch (London: Methuen, 1972), pp. lxvii-lxviii; and J.C. Maxwell, "The Name of Brutus," *Notes and Queries,* XIV (April 1967), p. 136.

10. Withycombe, p. 138.

11. Ibid., pp. 137-138.

12. See S. Schoenbaum, *Shakespeare's Lives* (Oxford: Oxford University Press, 1970), p. 26.

13. Edgar I. Fripp, *Shakespeare, Man and Artist* (Oxford: Oxford University Press, 1938), pp. 146-147.

14. A reprint of the first Quarto edition of *Hamlet* is edited by Albert B. Weiner (Great Neck, N.Y.: Barron's Educational Series, 1962).

15. "Othello's Name," *Notes and Queries,* N.S. VIII (April 1961), p. 139.

16. Ibid.

17. *Advice to an Author,* Part III, sect. 3, quoted in A New Variorum *Othello,* edited by H.H. Furness (Philadelphia: J.B. Lippincott, 1886), p. 57.

18. See Chapter 1, p. 22.

19. Knight, pp. 190-191.

20. See F.N. Lees, "Othello's Name," pp. 140-141.

21. Knight, p. 191.

22. See especially Clifford Stanley Sims, *The Origin and Signification of Scottish Surnames* (New York: Avenel Books, 1964).

23. Withycombe, p. 194.

24. Sims, p. 110.

25. See The New Arden *King Lear,* edited by Kenneth Muir (London: Methuen, 1952), p. xliiin.

26. See George Ferguson, *Signs and Symbols in Christian Art* (New York: Oxford University Press, 1961), p. 24.

27. The New Arden *King Lear,* p. 257. See S. Musgrove, "The Nomenclature of *King Lear," Review of English Studies,* VII (1956), p. 294-298.

28. Ibid., p. 5n.

29. Knight, p. 192.

30. Kokeritz, p. 61.

31. Robert Adger Law, "On Certain Proper Names in Shakespeare," *Texas Studies in English,* XXX (1951), p. 61-62.

32. Quoted from *Shakespeare's Plutarch,* edited by Walter W. Skeat (London: Macmillan, 1875), p. 304.

33. Law, "On Certain Proper Names in Shakespeare," p. 62.

34. See Knight, p. 195.

35. Ibid.

36. *Shakespeare's Plutarch,* p. 304.

37. *Dictionary of Classical Mythology,* edited by J.E. Zimmerman (New York: Bantam Books, 1971), pp. 284-285.

38. See The New Arden *Timon of Athens,* edited by H.J. Oliver (London: Methuen, 1969), p. 30n.

Notes to Chapter 4

1. See discussion of the sources in The New Arden *The Comedy of Errors,* edited by R.A. Foakes (London: Methuen, 1968), pp. xxiv-xxxiv; and *Narrative and Dramatic Sources of Shakespeare,* edited by Geoffrey Bullough (London: Routledge and Kegan Paul, 1957), I, pp. 3-11.

2. See note to "Induction," ii,93, in *The Riverside Shakespeare,* edited by G. Blakemore Evans *et al* (Boston: Houghton Mifflin, 1974), p. 113n.

3. Bullough, I, p. 61.

4. Florio: *biondello,* "such a one as we call a gouldilock."

5. The New Arden *The Two Gentlemen of Verona,* edited by Clifford Leech (London: Methuen, 1969), p. xxxix. The *Thyreus* suggestion is my own.

6. The modern edition is edited by Frances E. Richardson (Oxford: Early English Text Society, 1965).

7. The New Arden *The Two Gentlemen of Verona,* p. 2n.

8. The German *Julio and Hyppolita.* See ibid., pp. xxxix-xliv.

9. "What's in a Name?", in *The Sovereign Flower* (London: Methuen, 1958), p. 175.

10. The New Arden *The Two Gentlemen of Verona,* p. xxxix.

11. See Bullough, I, pp. 428-430, for relevant history about the King of Navarre.

12. Warburton is quoted in The New Arden *Love's Labor's Lost,* edited by Richard David (London: Methuen, 1968), p. xxxiii.

13. Fleay's conjecture. Ibid., p. xxxiv.

14. See Bullough, I, pp. 367-376.

15. Quoted in ibid., p. 371.

16. Ibid., p. 369.

17. Ibid., p. 370.

18. A New Variorum Edition of *A Midsummer Night's Dream,* edited by H.H. Furness (New York: Dover, 1963), has a wonderful note which I should like to quote in full: "We would be grateful to editors if they would only tell us why the *'name'* of Demetrius should be thus referred to. Is there a covert reference to *demit,* i.e. to humble, to subject, or to *meat* which is stuck on a spit?" So questioned the German scholar Tiessen in 1877. To

which Furness replies: "*i.e.* 'De-meat-rius,' I suppose. This insight of the way in which a learned German reads his Shakespeare would be interesting if it were not so depressing," p. 110.

19. See A New Variorum Edition of *A Midsummer Night's Dream*, pp. 289-296.

20. Ibid.

21. Ibid., p. 1n.

22. *Shakespeare Our Contemporary* (Garden City, N.Y.: Anchor Books, 1966), pp. 218-223.

23. Bullough, I, p. 445.

24. See George Ferguson, *Signs and Symbols in Christian Art* (New York: Oxford University Press, 1961), pp. 104-105; and E.G. Withycombe, *The Oxford Dictionary of English Christian Names* (Oxford: Oxford University Press, 1973), p. 26.

25. Ferguson, p. 105.

26. Knight's suggestion, pp. 176-177.

27. The New Arden *The Merchant of Venice*, edited by John Russell Brown (New York: Random House, 1964), p. 9n.

28. Knight's suggestion, p. 171.

29. Withycombe, p. 39.

30. See The New Arden *The Merchant of Venice*, p. 3.

31. Ibid.

32. Robert F. Fleissner, "A Key to the Name Shylock," *American Notes and Queries*, IV (December 1966), pp. 52-54.

33. Norman Nathan, "Three Notes on *The Merchant of Venice*," *Shakespeare Association Bulletin*, XXIII (1948), p. 152-154.

34. The New Arden *The Merchant of Venice*, p. 3.

35. See C.S. Lewis, *English Literature in the Sixteenth Century* (New York: Oxford University Press, 1954), pp. 310-311.

36. The New Arden *The Merry Wives of Windsor*, edited by H.J. Oliver (London: Methuen, 1971), pp. xxxiv-xxxv.

37. Withycombe, p. xxviii.

38. See Norman N. Holland, *Psychoanalysis and Shakespeare* (New York: McGraw-Hill, 1966), p. 202.

39. "Punning Names in Shakespeare," *Modern Language Notes*, LXV (April 1950), p. 241.

40. "Hero's Name-and Namesake-in *Much Ado About Nothing*," *English Language Notes* (March 1970), pp. 175-179.

41. "The Names in *As You Like It*," *The Shakespeare Association Bulletin*, XV (1940), p. 255.

42. (Berlin: Reimer, 1841), pp. 240,332.

43. Tannenbaum, p. 256.

44. Bullough, II, p. 15.

45. The association is noted by Camden in *Remaines*, p. 44. Also, as French's conjecture in A New Variorum Edition of *As You Like It*, edited by H.H. Furness (Philadelphia: Lippincott, 1918), p. 2n.

46. Tannenbaum, p. 256.

47. Ibid.; and Withycombe, p. 34.

48. William M. Jones, "William Shakespeare as William in *As You Like It*," *Shakespeare Quarterly*, XI (Spring 1960), pp. 228-231.

49. Tannenbaum, p. 256.

50. Withycombe, p. 294.

51. See Leslie Hotson, *The First Night of "Twelfth Night"* (London: Rupert Hart-Davis, 1954), pp. 11-65.

52. See ibid., pp. 93-119.

53. See Leslie Hotson, *Shakespeare's Motley* (New York: Haskell House, 1952), pp. 120-121.

54. Ferguson, p. 24.

55. *Shakespeare and the Comedy of Forgiveness* (New York: Columbia University Press, 1965), p. 114.

56. *The Riverside Shakespeare*, p. 525n.

57. "On Certain Proper Names in Shakespeare," *Texas Studies in English*, XXX (1951), p. 64.

58. Ibid.

59. "Shakespeare and Erasmus," *Notes and Queries*, N.S., III (October 1956), p. 424.

60. See Bullough, II, pp. 430-442.

61. "*Measure for Measure* and Christian Doctrine of the Atonement," *PMLA*, LXI (1946), p. 1035.

62. "Comic Form in *Measure for Measure*," in *Shakespeare Survey 8*, edited by Allardyce Nicoll (Cambridge: Cambridge University Press, 1955), p. 24.

63. See Mark Eccles, "Barnabe Barnes," in *Thomas Lodge and Other Elizabethans*, edited by Charles J. Sisson (Cambridge, Mass.: Harvard University Press, 1933), pp. 165-243.

64. See Bullough, II, pp. 524-530.

65. The New Arden *Measure for Measure*, edited by J.W. Lever (New York: Random House, 1967), p. 114n.

66. See Ibid., pp. xlviii-li.

67. See *The Catholic Encyclopedia* (New York: The Encyclopedia Press, 1909), V, pp. 389-391.

68. See The New Arden *Pericles*, edited by F.D. Hoeniger (London: Methuen, 1969), pp. xiii-xxiii.

69. Two of Shakespeare's eighteenth-century editors, George Steevens and Edmond Malone, believed this, as did George Lyman Kittredge in our own time.

70. J.M.S. Tompkins, "Why Pericles?", *Review of English Studies* N.S., III (October 1952), pp. 322-324.

71. *Shakespeare's Ovid*, edited by W.H.D. Rouse (London: De La More Press, 1904), p. 250.

72. The New Arden *Pericles*, p. 3.

73. Noted by Hoeniger, ibid., p. xviii.

74. See *Dictionary of Classical Mythology*, edited by J.E. Zimmerman (New York: Bantam Books, 1971), p. 261.

75. Withycombe, pp. 196-198; see also *The New Catholic Encyclopedia* (New York: McGraw-Hill, 1967), IX, pp. 199-200.

76. See *A Concise Etymological Dictionary of the English*

Language, edited by Walter W. Skeat (New York: Capricorn, 1963), p. 391.

77. *Johnson on Shakespeare,* edited by Arthur Sherbo (New Haven, Conn.: Yale University Press, 1968), II, p. 908.

78. *Shakespearean Criticism,* edited by T.M. Raysor (London: Dent, 1960), I, p. 37.

79. See The New Arden *Cymbeline,* edited by James Nosworthy (London: Methuen, 1969), pp. xxii-xxiii; and Bullough, VII, p. 18.

80. Knight, pp. 196-197.

81. Ibid., p. 197.

82. Many have noted this. See, for example, Withycombe, pp. 161-162.

83. Ibid.

84. The New Arden *The Winter's Tale,* edited by J.H.P. Pafford (London: Methuen, 1963), p. 164.

85. Knight, p. 197.

86. The New Arden *Cymbeline,* p. 138n.

87. The New Arden *The Winter's Tale,* p. 163; and Law, "On Certain Proper Names in Shakespeare," pp. 62-63.

88. See Withycombe, p. 185.

89. *Shakespeare's Ovid,* p. 226.

90. "that which is lost." See The New Arden *The Winter's Tale,* p. 164.

91. See The New Arden *The Tempest,* edited by Frank Kermode (New York: Random House, 1964), pp. 142-145.

92. Two suggestions among many. Ibid., p. xxxviiin.

93. Knight, p. 198.

94. Quoted from Bullough, VIII, p. 257.

95. Knight, p. 188.

96. Withycombe, pp. 16-17.

Notes to Chapter 5

1. Lines 445-447. Not everyone agrees with Edmond Malone that these lines do indeed refer to Shakespeare. See S. Schoenbaum, *Shakespeare's Lives* (Oxford: Oxford University Press, 1970), pp. 242-243.

2. Quoted from the unpaged first edition.

3. Schoenbaum, p. 735.

4. *Review of English Studies* (February 1970), pp. 41-48.

5. See discussion in The New Arden *The First Part of King Henry IV,* edited by A.R. Humphreys (London: Methuen, 1960), pp. xv-xviii.

6. Quoted in Leslie Hotson, *Shakespeare's Sonnets Dated* (London: Rupert Hart-Davis, 1949), p. 147.

7. Ibid., pp. 147-160.

8. Quoted in *The Shakespeare Allusion Book,* edited by John Munro (New York: Duffield, 1909), p. 88.

9. See discussion in The New Arden *The Merry Wives of Windsor,* edited by H.J. Oliver (London: Methuen, 1971), pp. xliv-lviii.

10. Quoted in *The Shakespeare Allusion Book,* p. 219. Some also see an allusion to Shakespeare the actor playing the King's part in George Peele's *Edward I:* "Shake thy spears in honor of his name,/ Under whose royalty thou wearest the same."

11. See Roland Mushat Frye, *Shakespeare's Life and Times* (Princeton, N.J.: Princeton University Press, 1967), illus. 68.

12. Frye sees in the illustration a similarity with actor John Lowin (1576-1669?), who perhaps played the part of Falstaff for Shakespeare's company and was still alive when the engraving was made.

INDEX